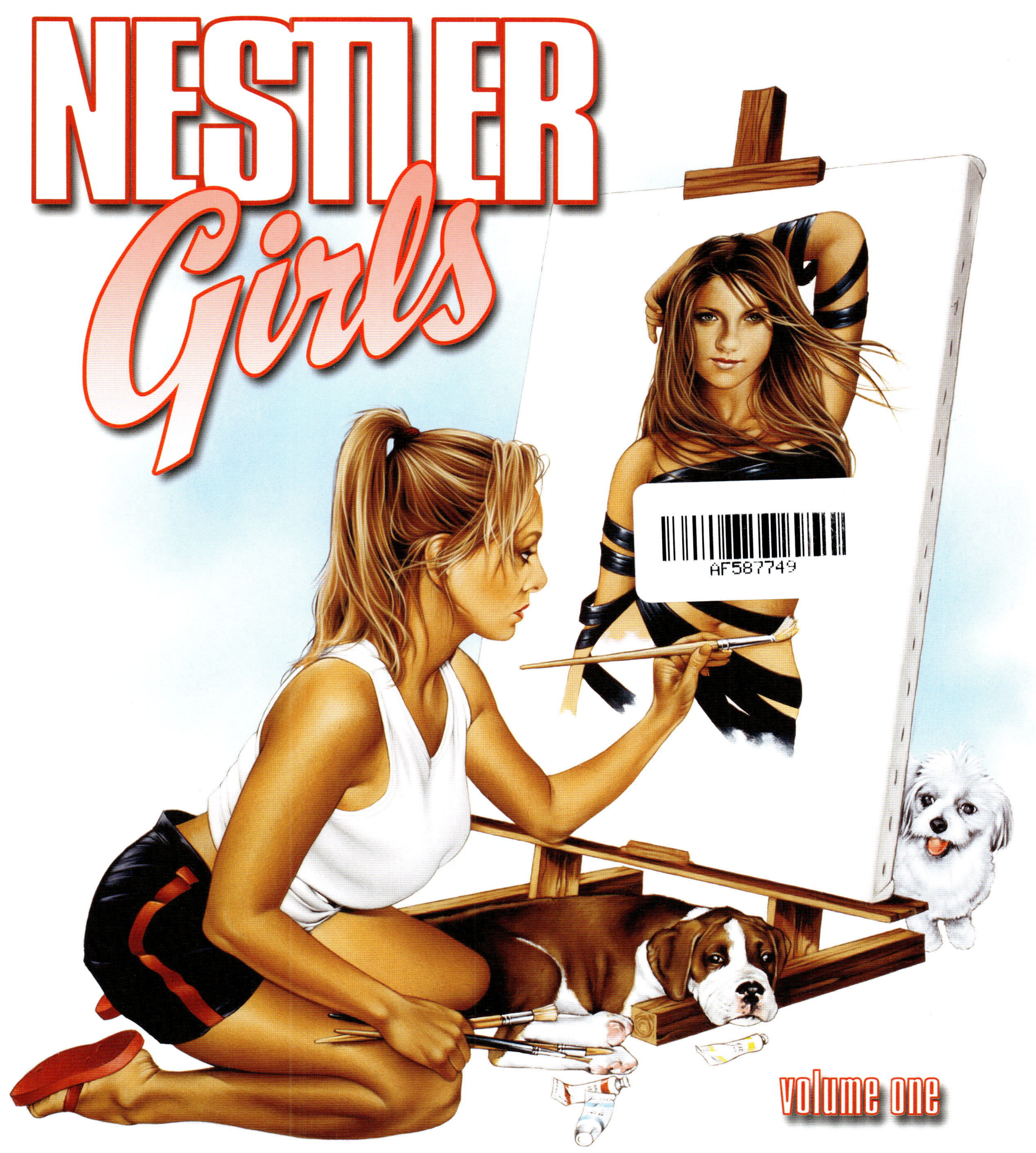

AN SQP PRESENTATION

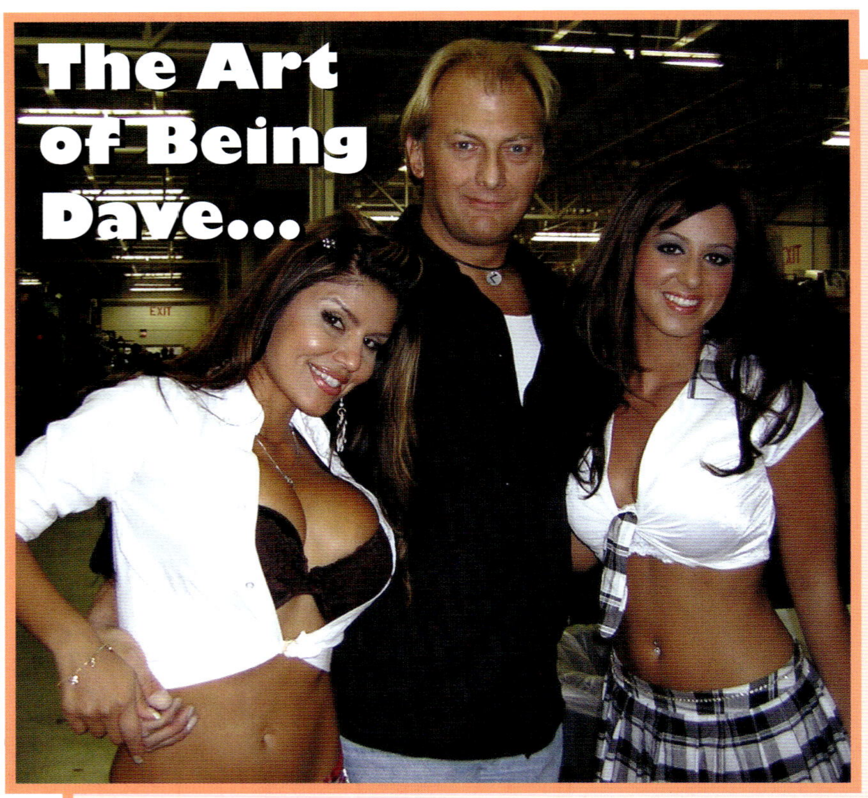

The Art of Being Dave...

You know you've arrived in the world of popular art when your name creates an immediate image in someone's mind. Say "Alberto Vargas", and suddenly all the long-legged pin-up fantasies that kept American soldiers company throughout World War II come forth. Mention "Frank Frazetta", and a bevy of round-rumped girls are fleeing the advances of knuckle-dragging cavemen. Whisper "Hajime Sorayama", and robotic sex-droids dripping motor oil glide into view. Well, it's finally gotten to the point where you can say "Dave Nestler", and all the state-of-the-art fantasy girls of the 21st Century come front and center for review! His girls are apple-pie sweet and burn-your-mouth spicy, which explains both his appreciative audience and our 4th collaboration with the good Mister Nestler!

Dave is meticulous in his preparation and generous with his time. Especially with the models that he uses to create the paintings he's so well known for. The mark of a true professional, he'll spend untold hours with nude and semi-nude young ladies, just to get all the details and subtle nuances needed to get the job done right. What a guy! That's dedication! Seriously, Dave is also known for his generosity towards other artists, both pro and aspiring illustrators. Offering advice and info on everything from acrylic painting techniques to the ins and outs of the business side of the pinup market. His "Hot Babe" subject matter has naturally made him a favorite among the Rock & Roll, tattoo, and motorhead crowd. As for what he's done for the image of Catholic School Girls, let's just say enrollment isn't the only thing that's gone up! If you're a fan of Dave's, this new collection will be a welcome addition to your art library. If you're new to the Nestler girls, boy - are you in for some non-stop fun!

Always a pleasure to print perfection!
Sal Quartuccio
Bob Keenan
Publishers

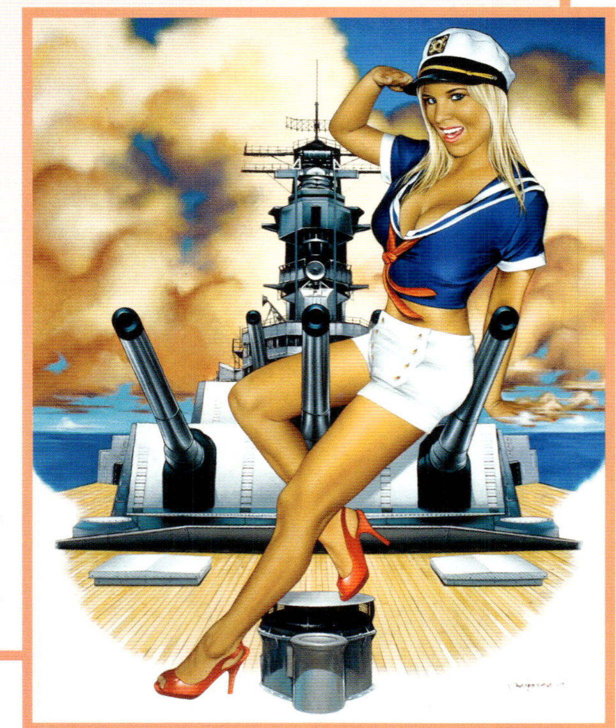

Nestler Girls Volume One

Book design by Grassy Knoll Studios.

Published by
SQP Inc.
PO Box 248 - Columbus, NJ 08022

Sal Quartuccio & Bob Keenan - Publishers

For a free full color catalog showcasing the entire SQP line of erotic, fantasy, and pin-up artwork, go to:
www.sqpinc.com

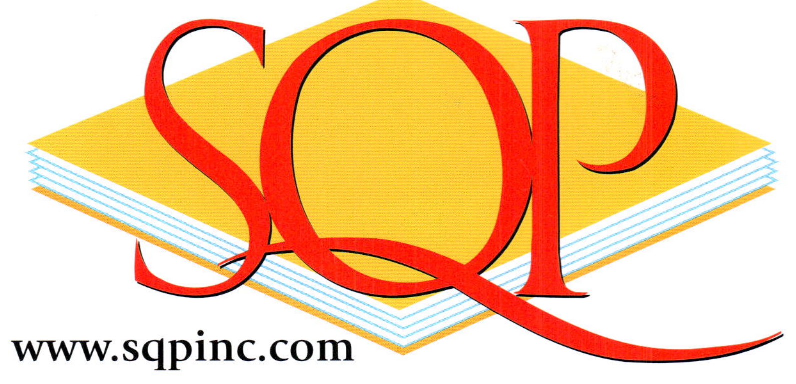

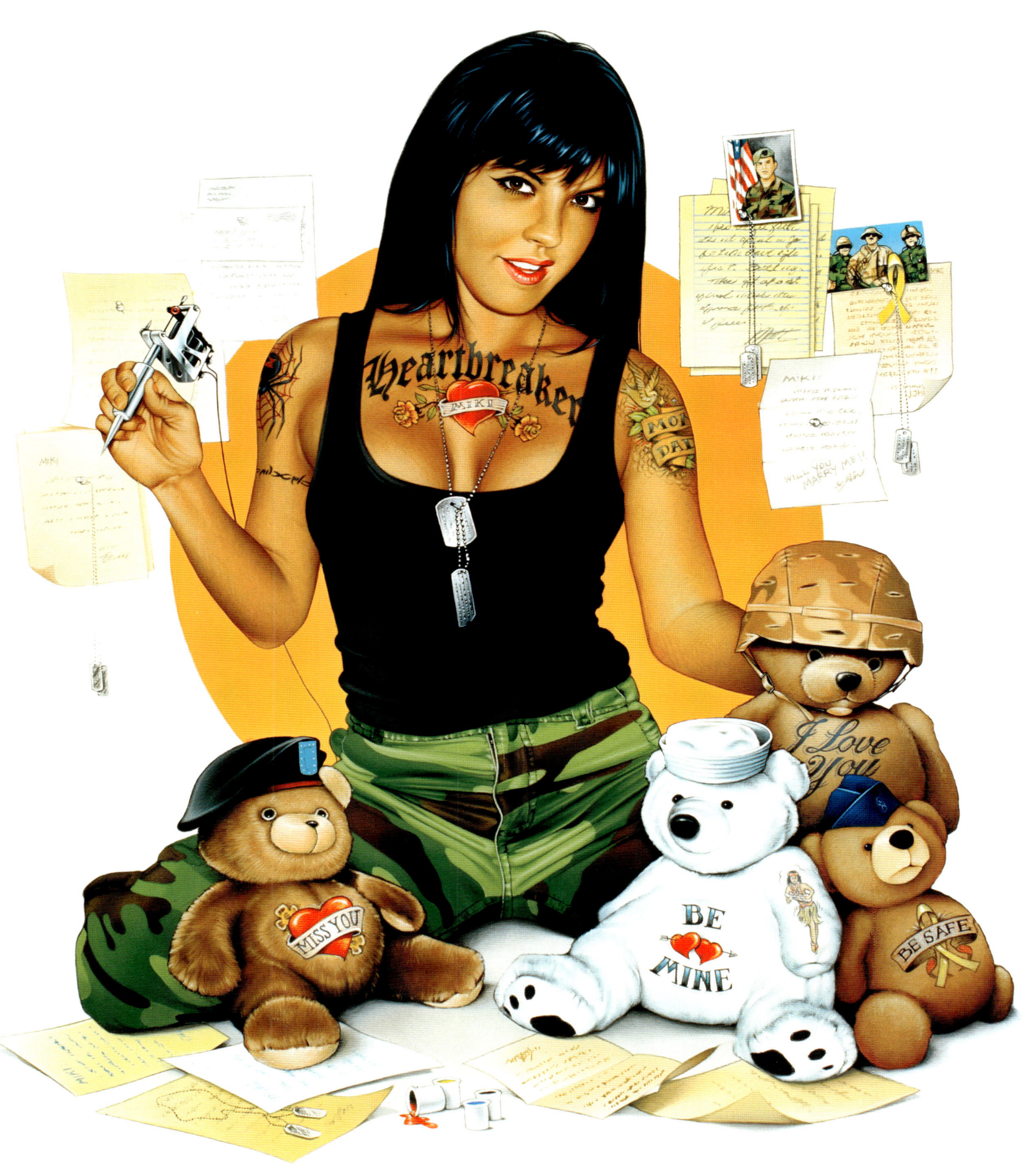
Heartbreaker
MIKI
MOM
DAD
I Love You
MISS YOU
BE
MINE
BE SAFE
MIKI
WILL YOU MARRY ME!!

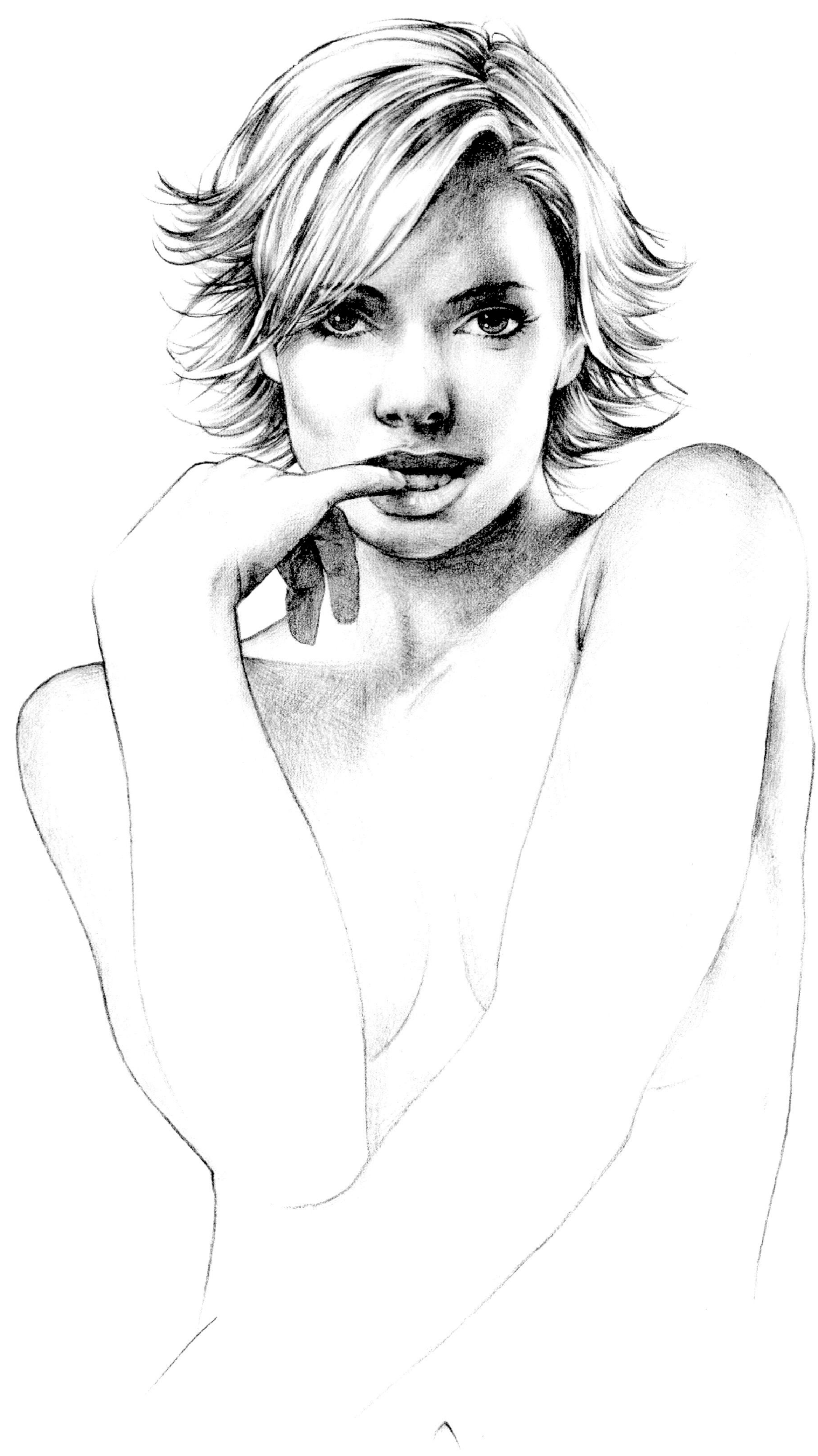

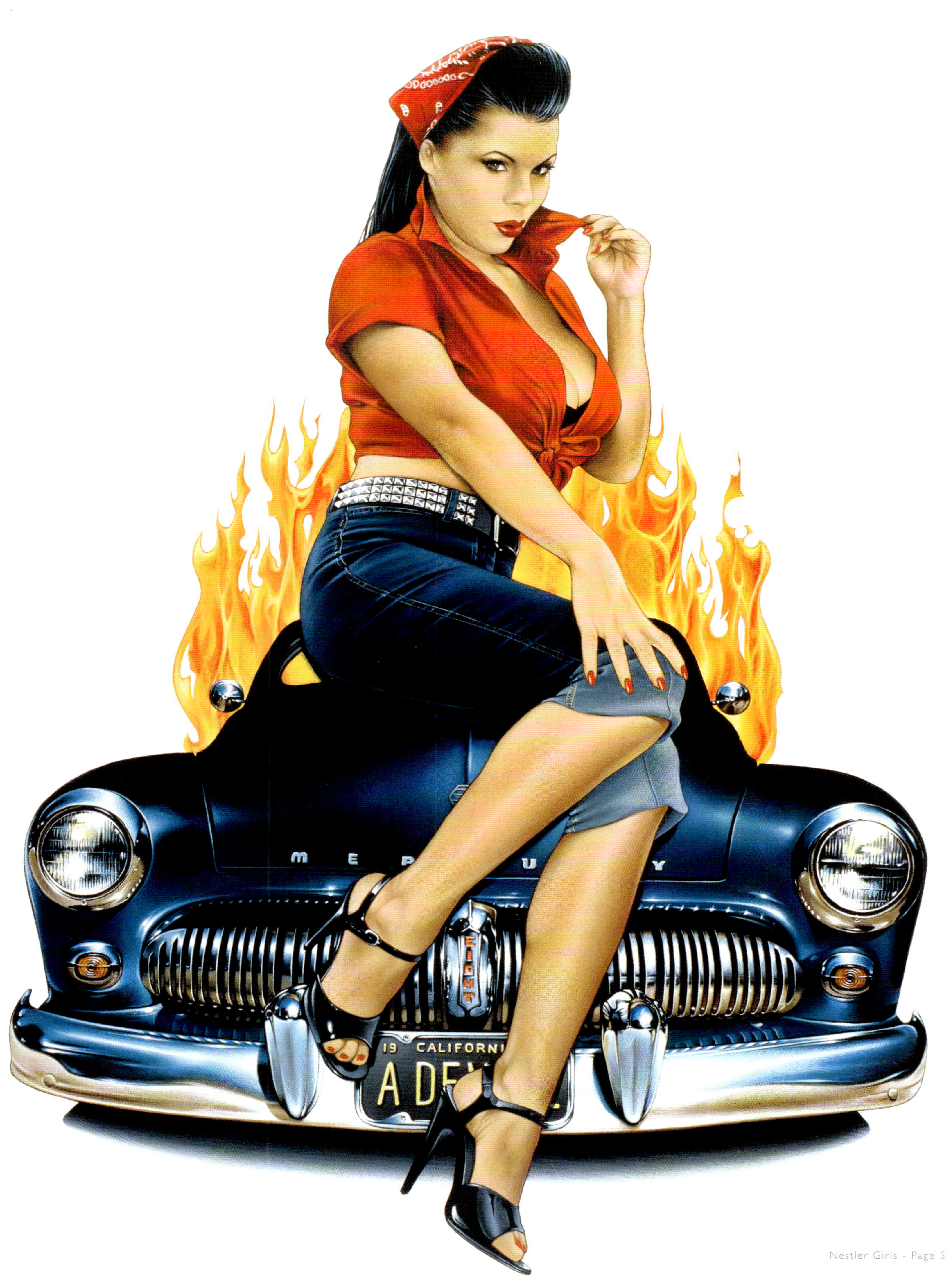
EIGHT
19

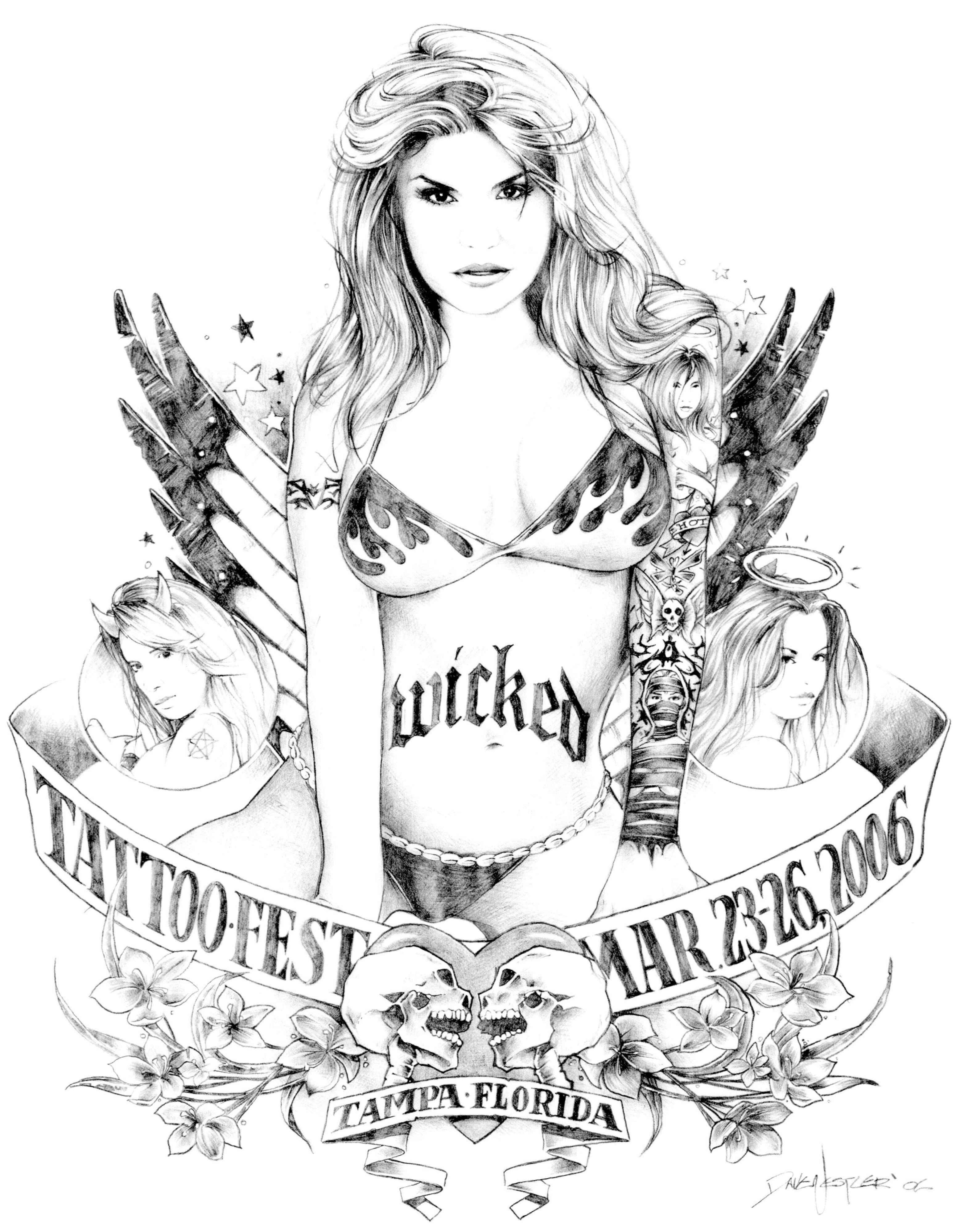
wicked
HOT
TATTOO·FEST
MAR 23-26, 2006
TAMPA·FLORIDA

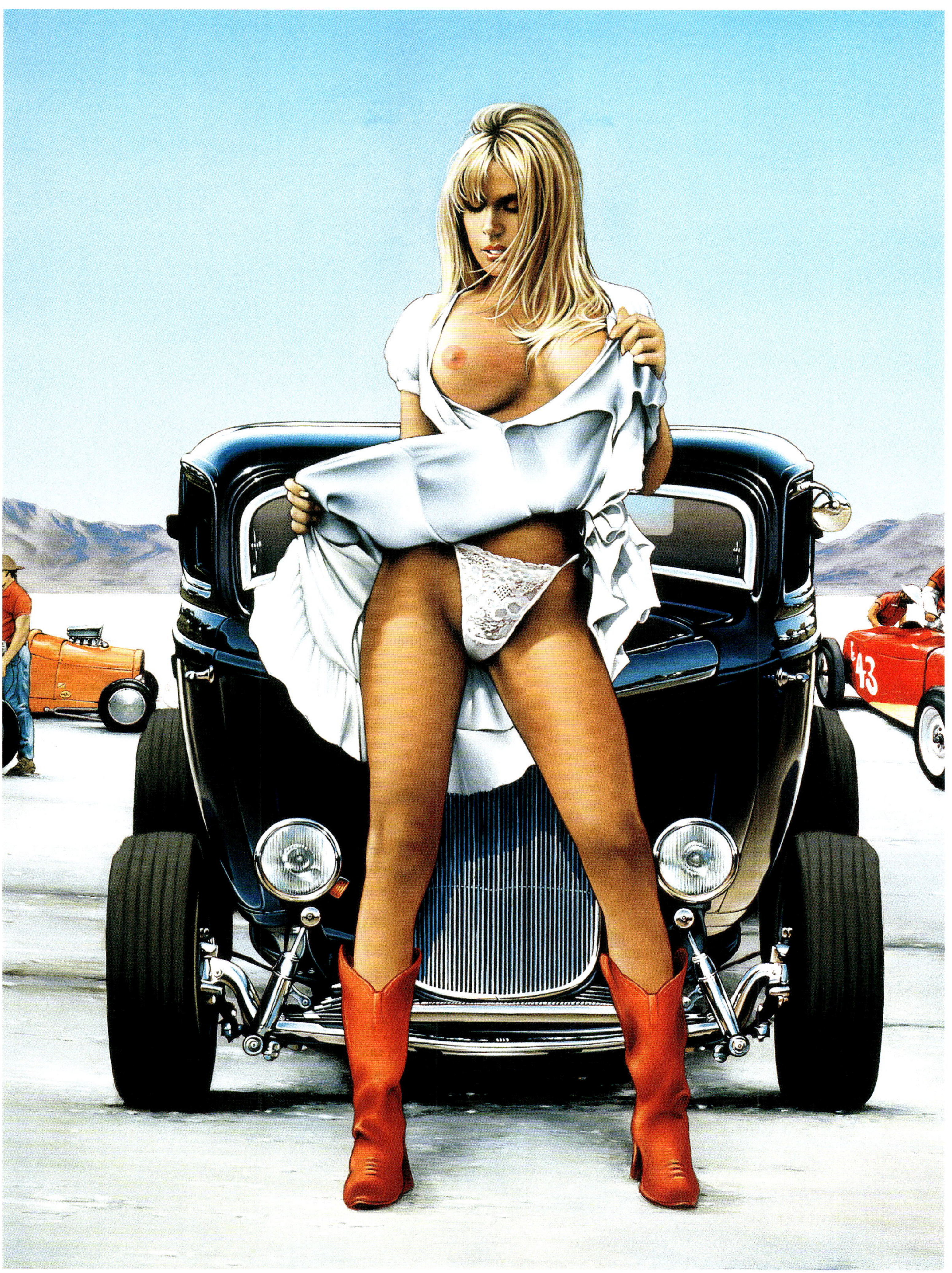
43

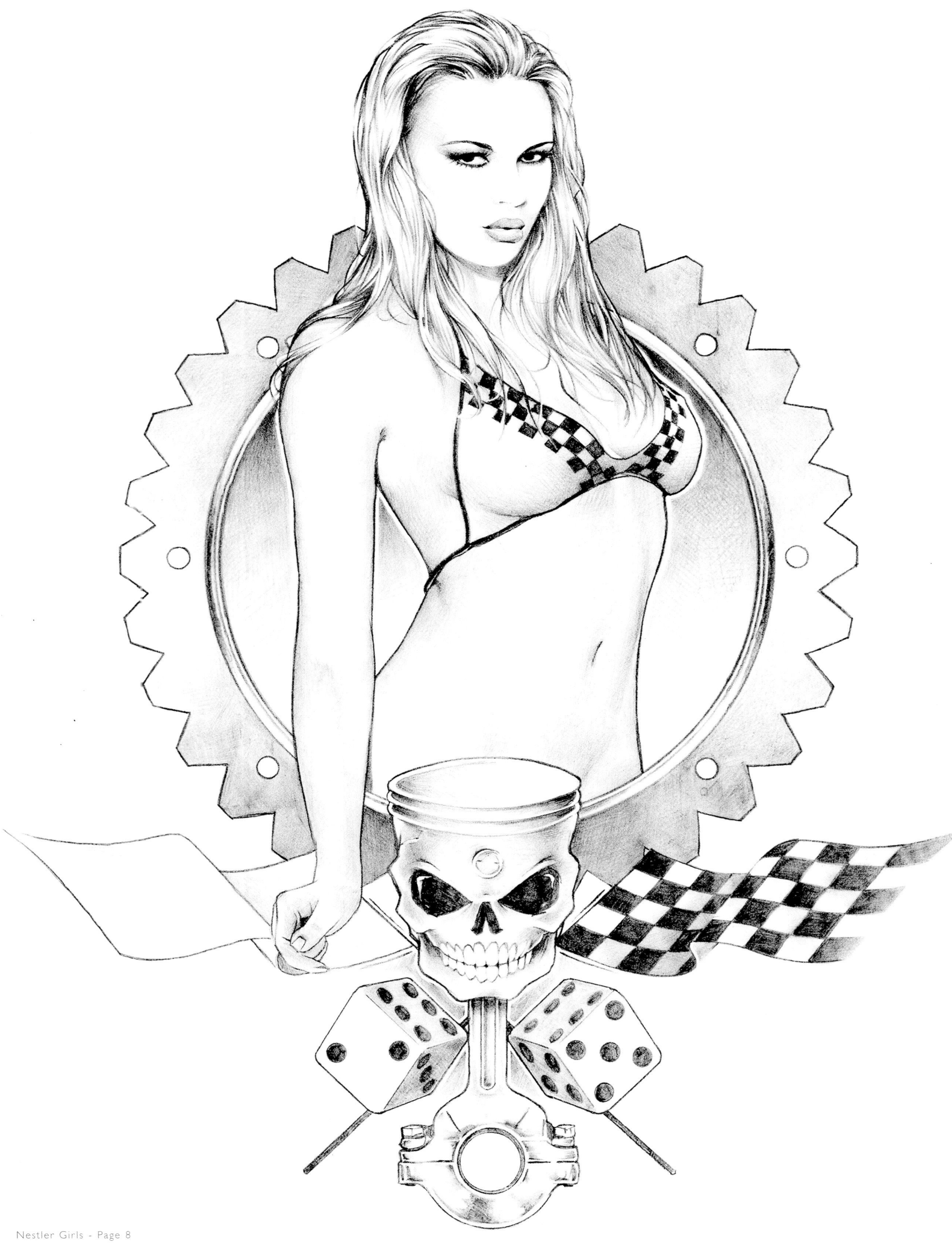

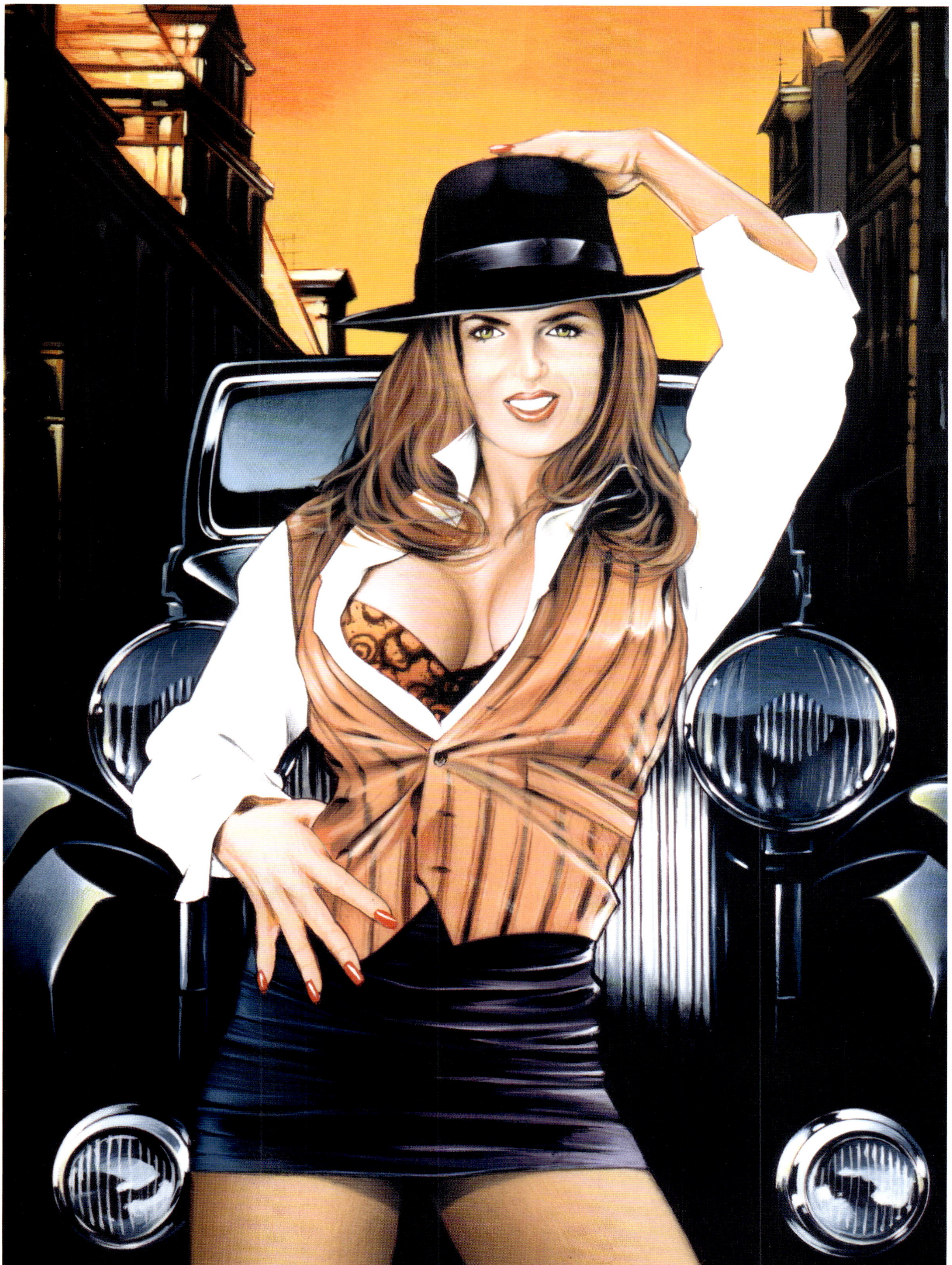

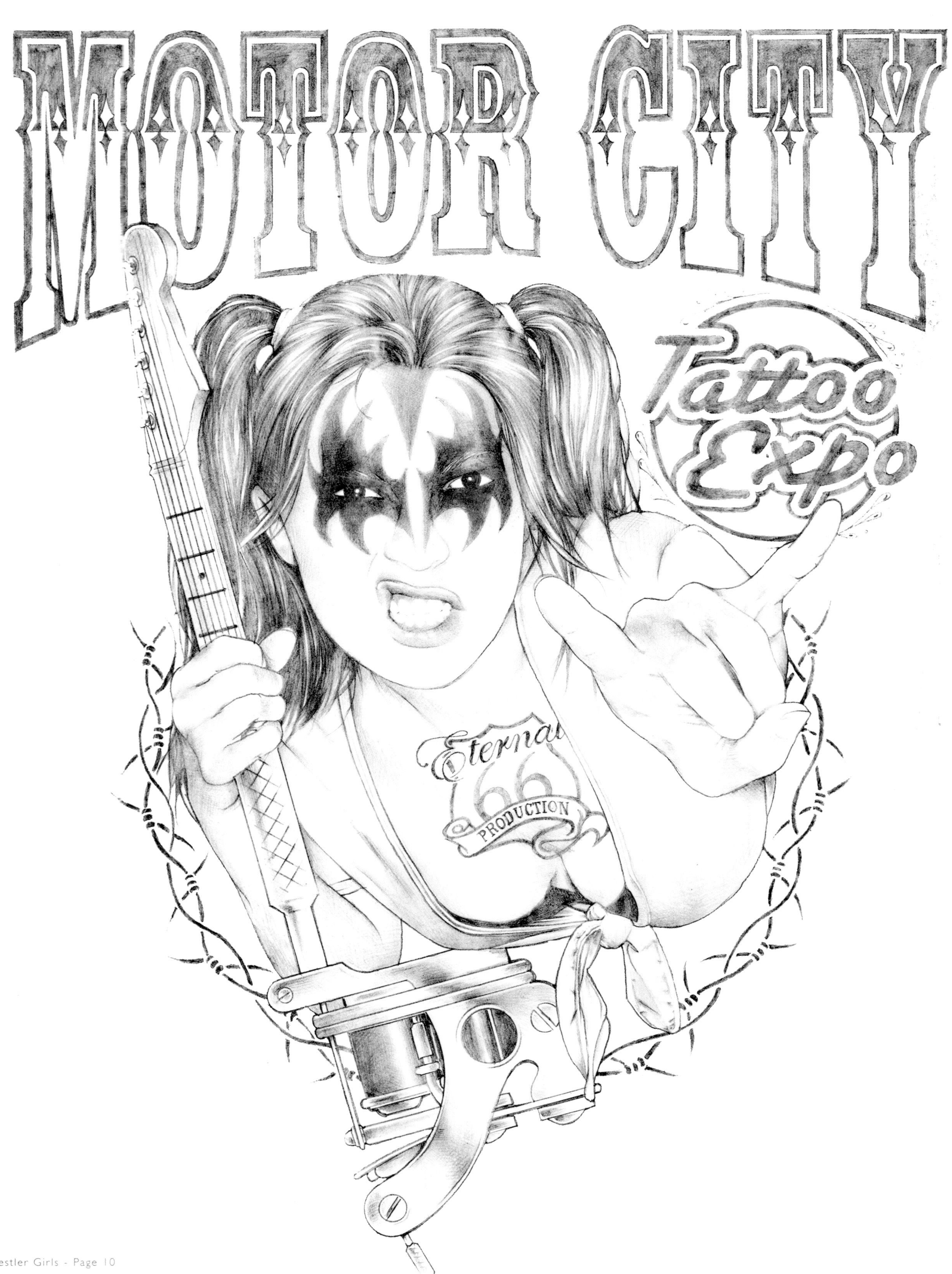
MOTOR CITY
Tattoo Expo
Eternal
66
PRODUCTION

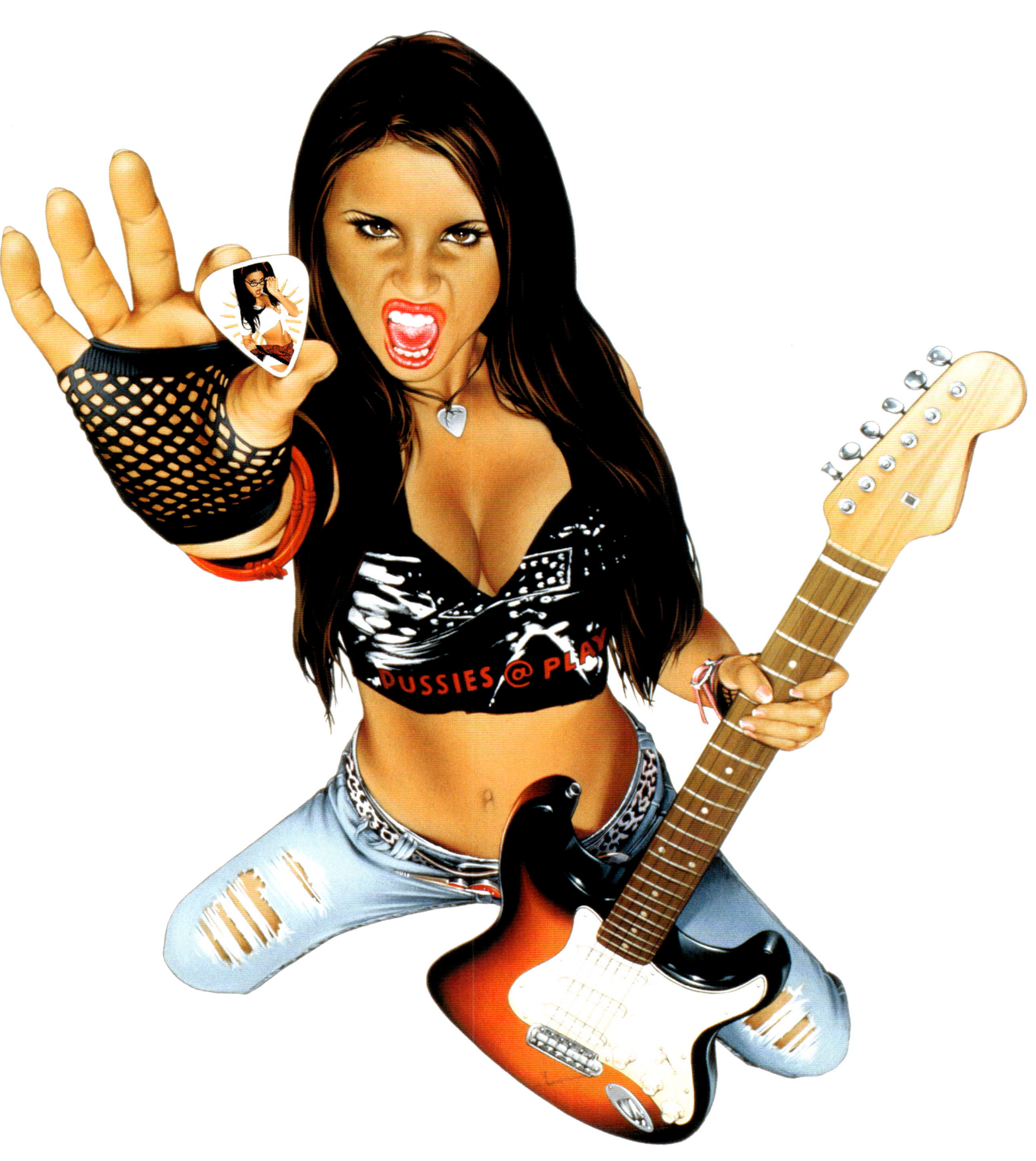
PUSSIES @ PLAY

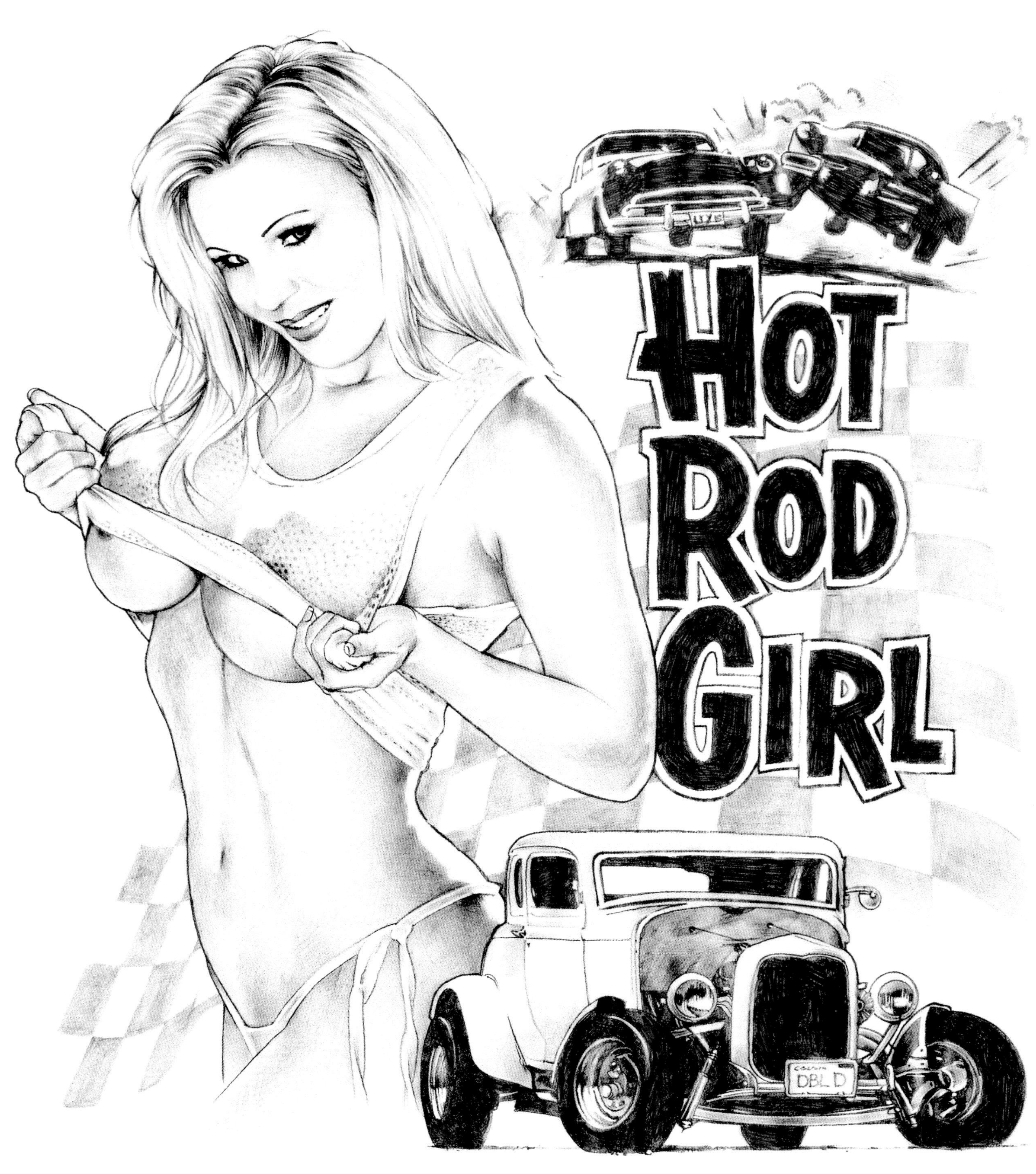
HOT
ROD
GIRL
DBL D

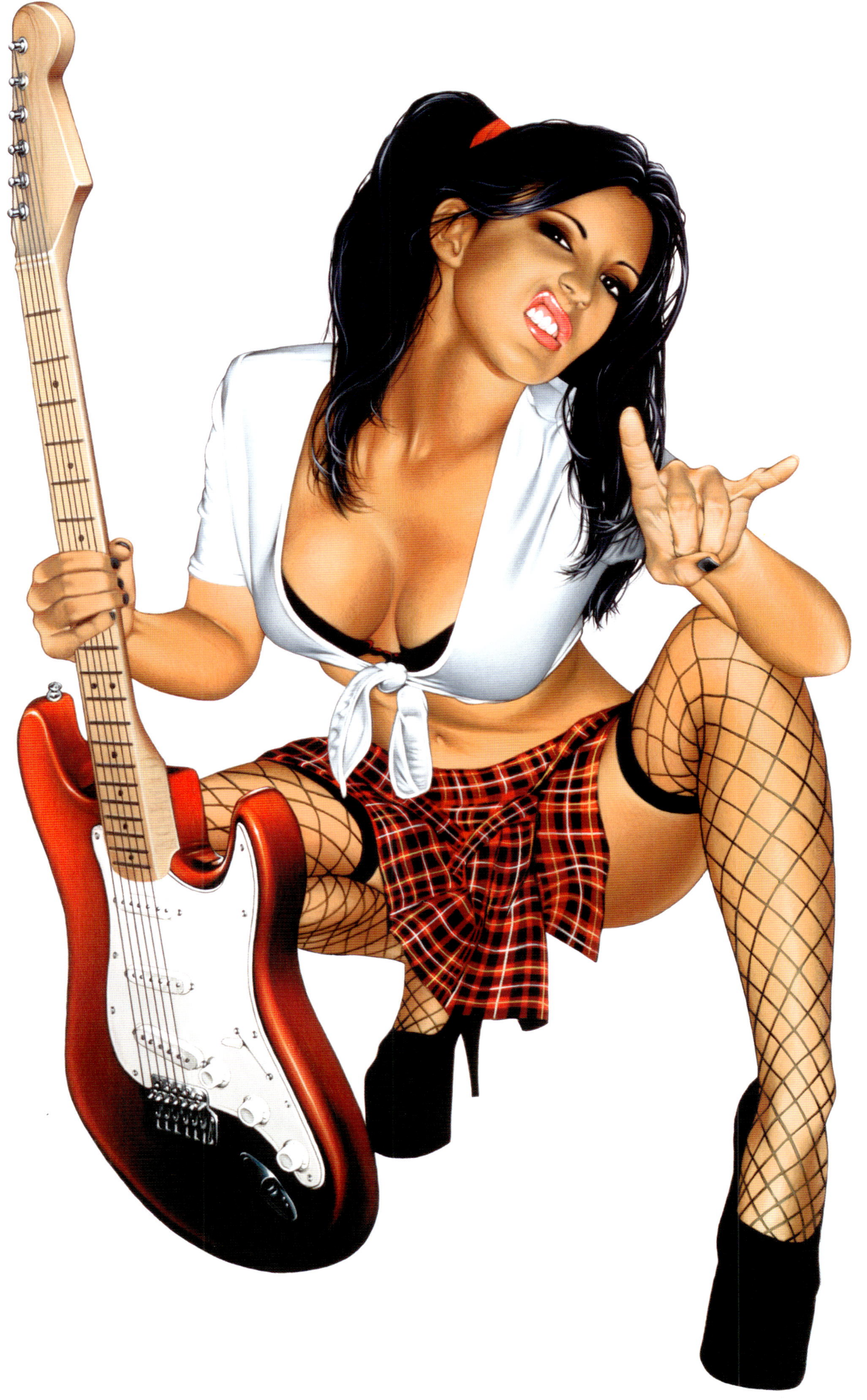

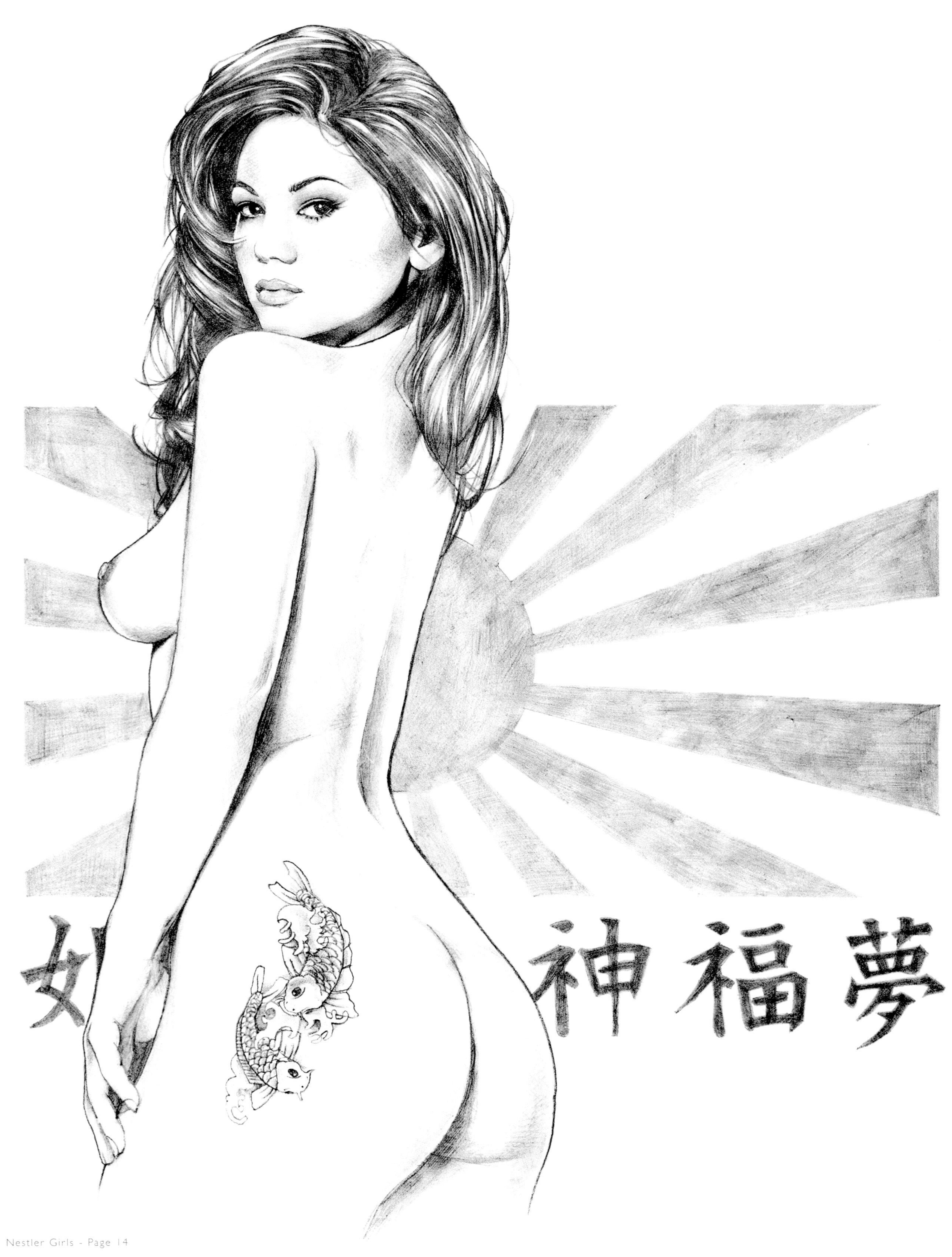
神福夢

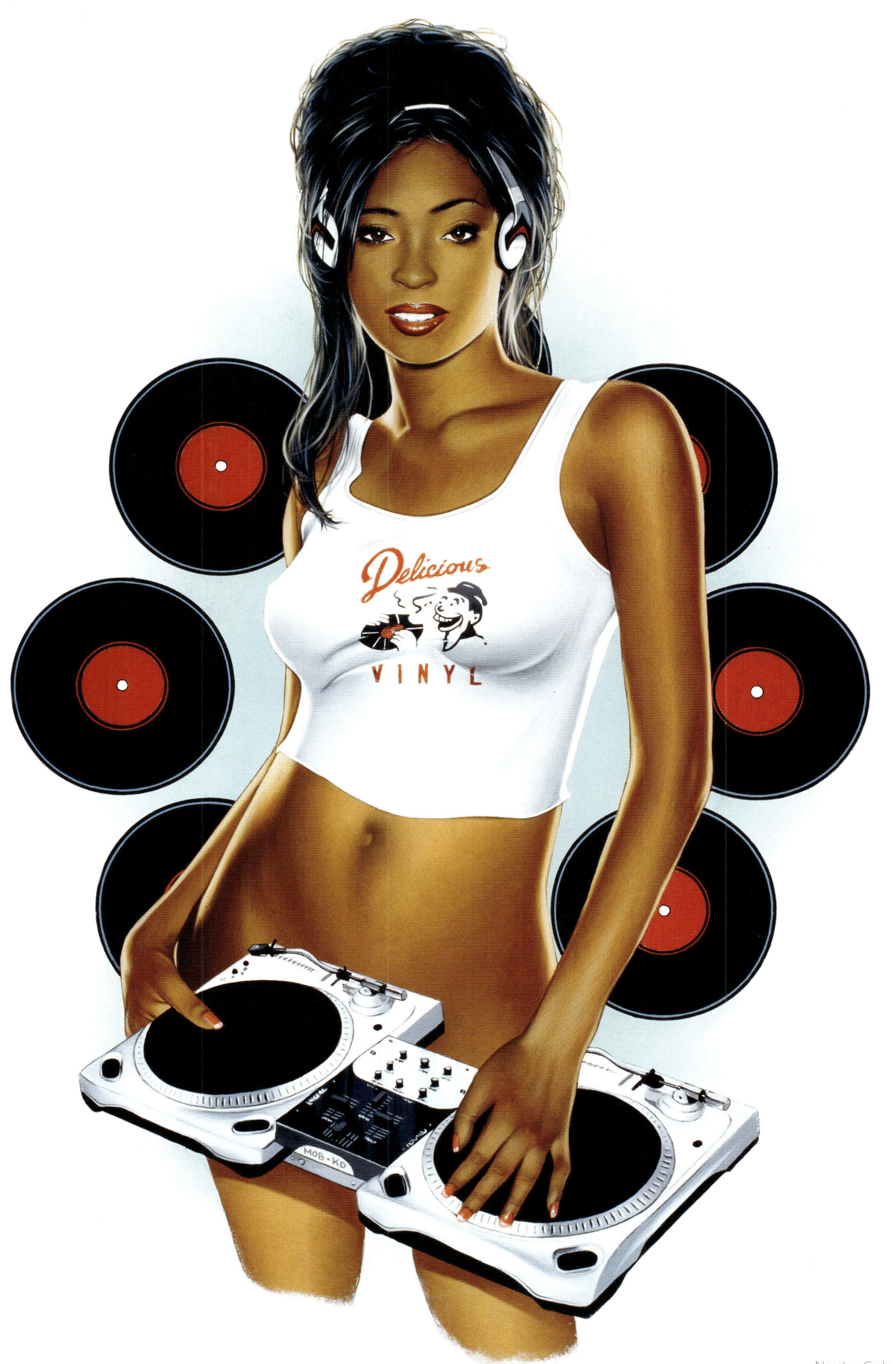
Delicious
VINYL
MOB-KD

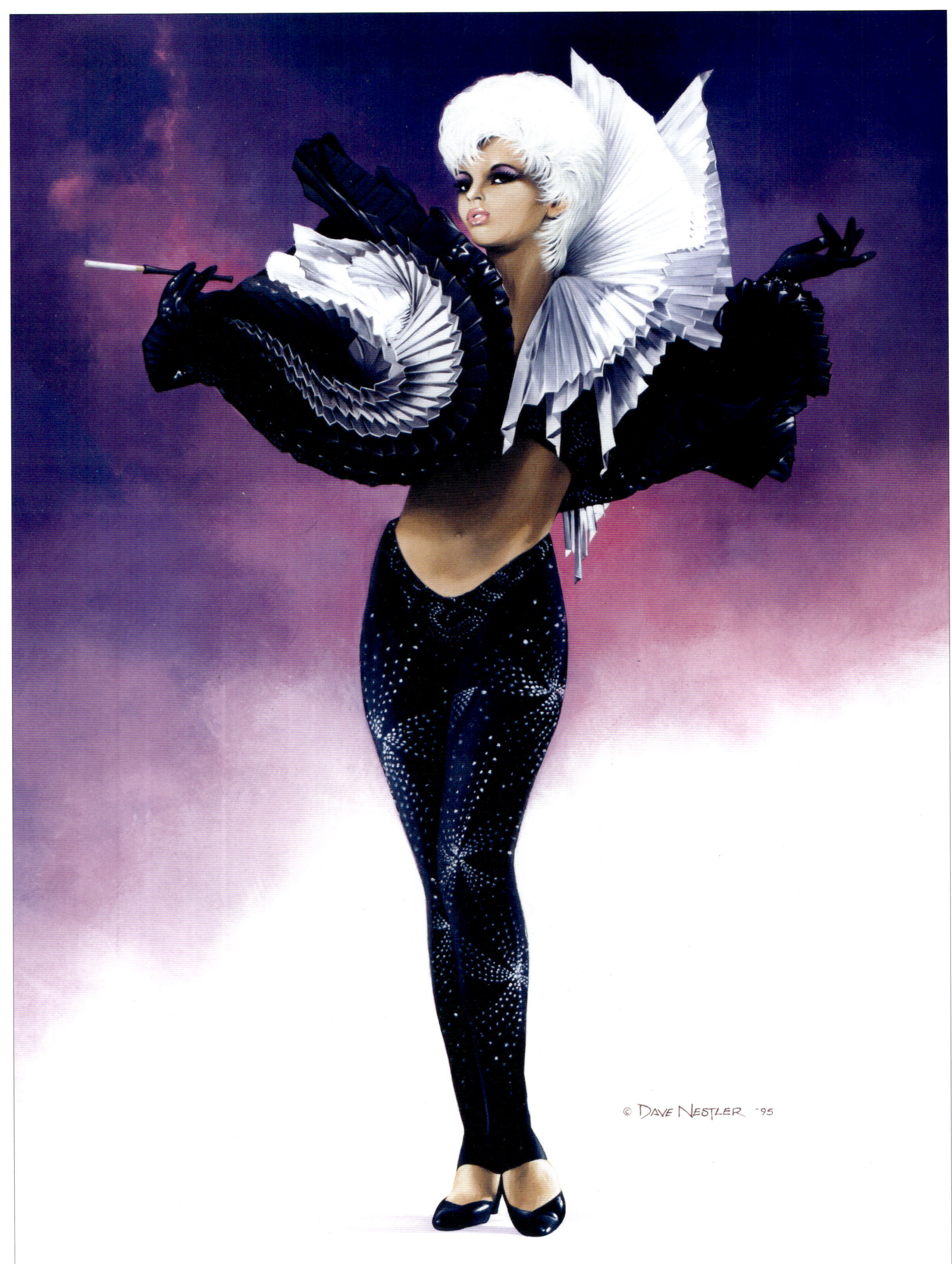
© DAVE NESTLER '95

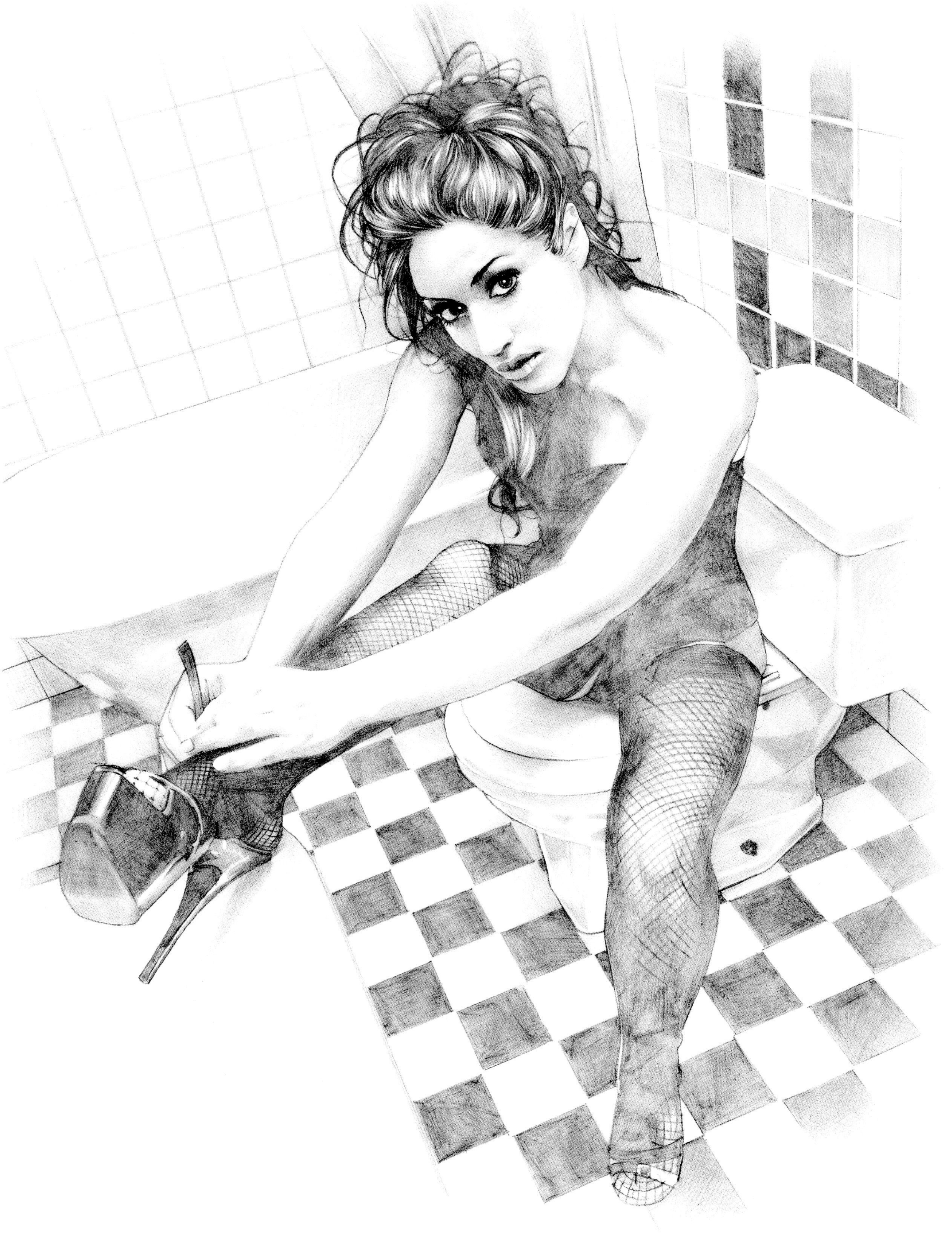

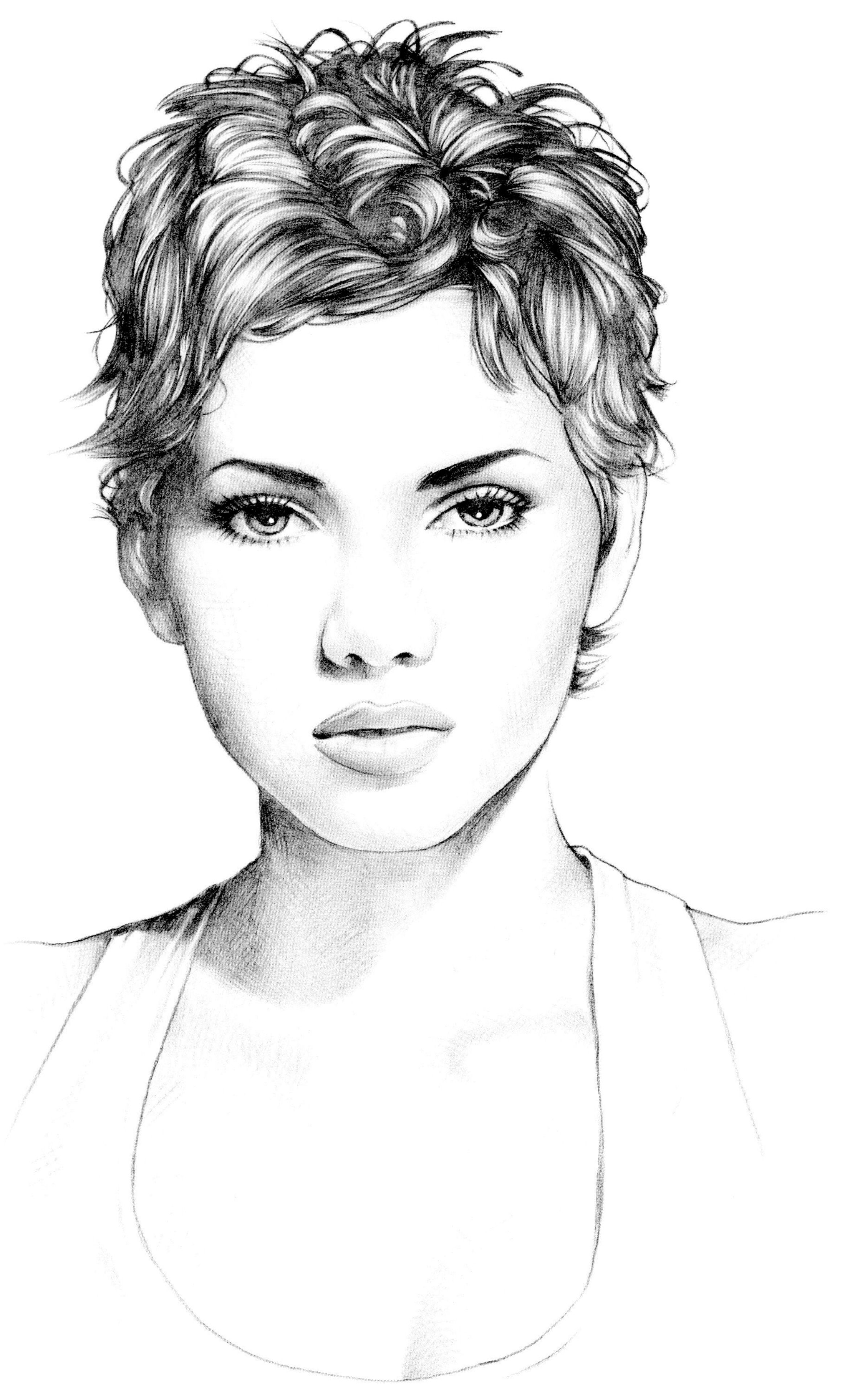

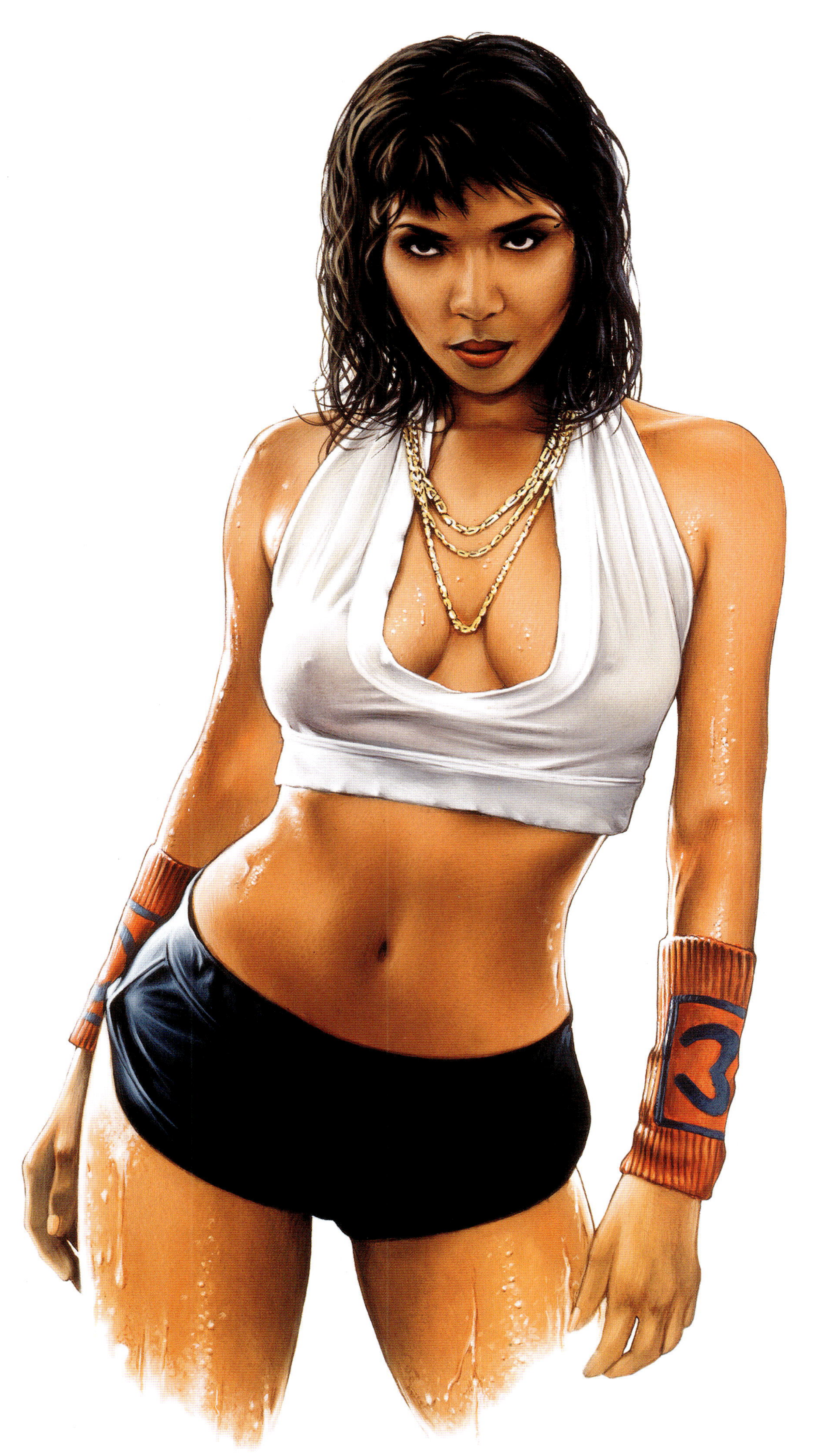

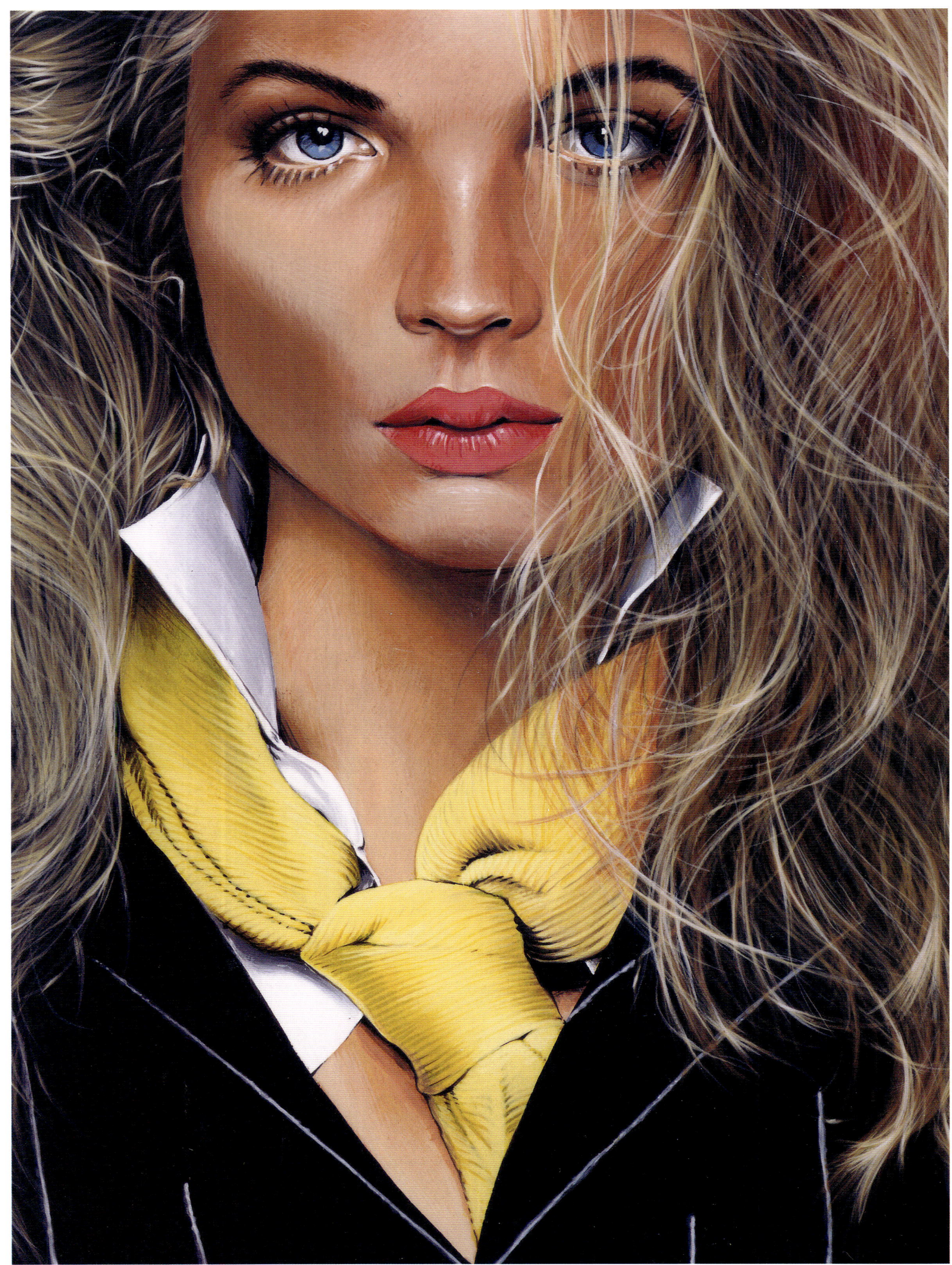

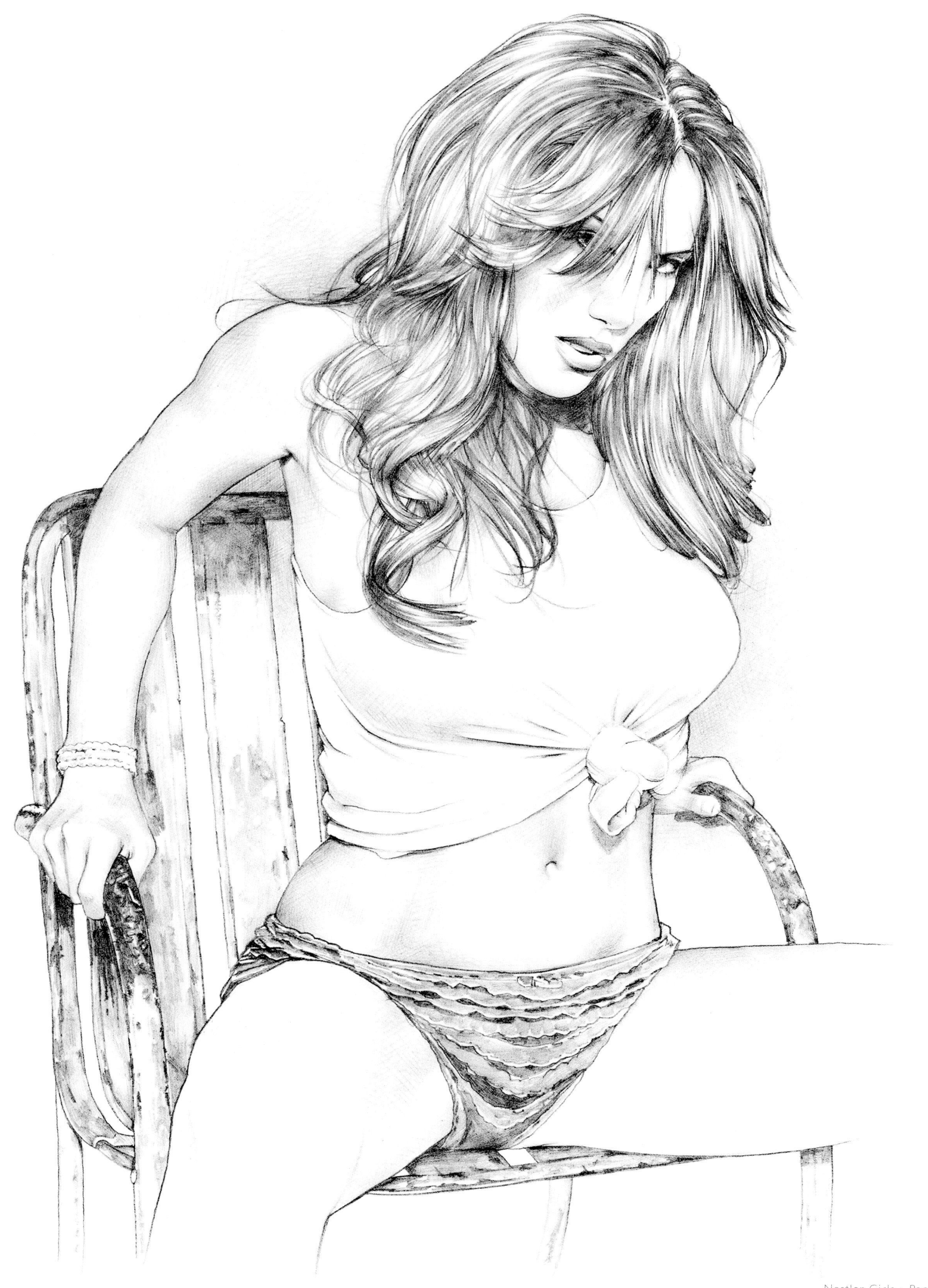

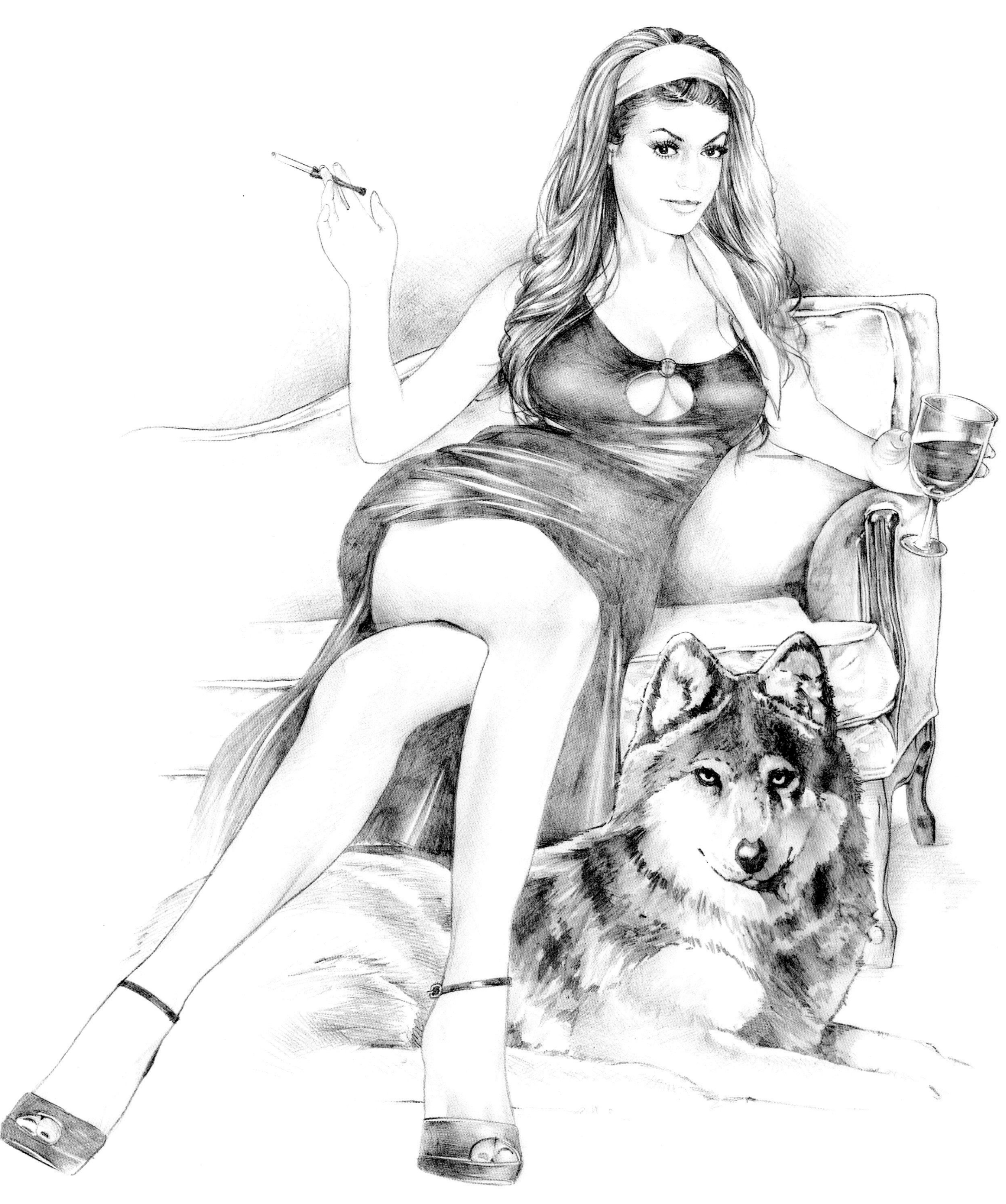

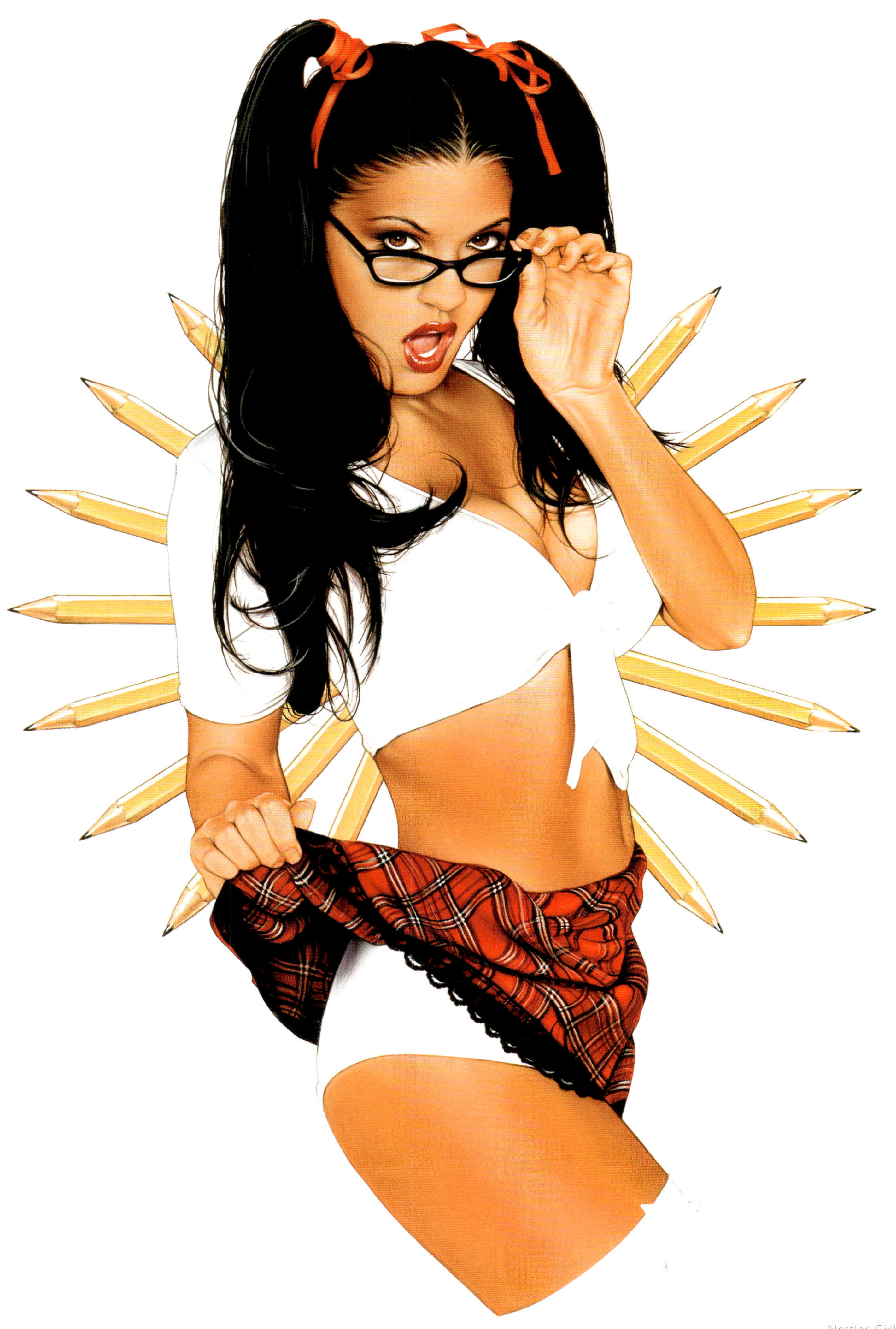

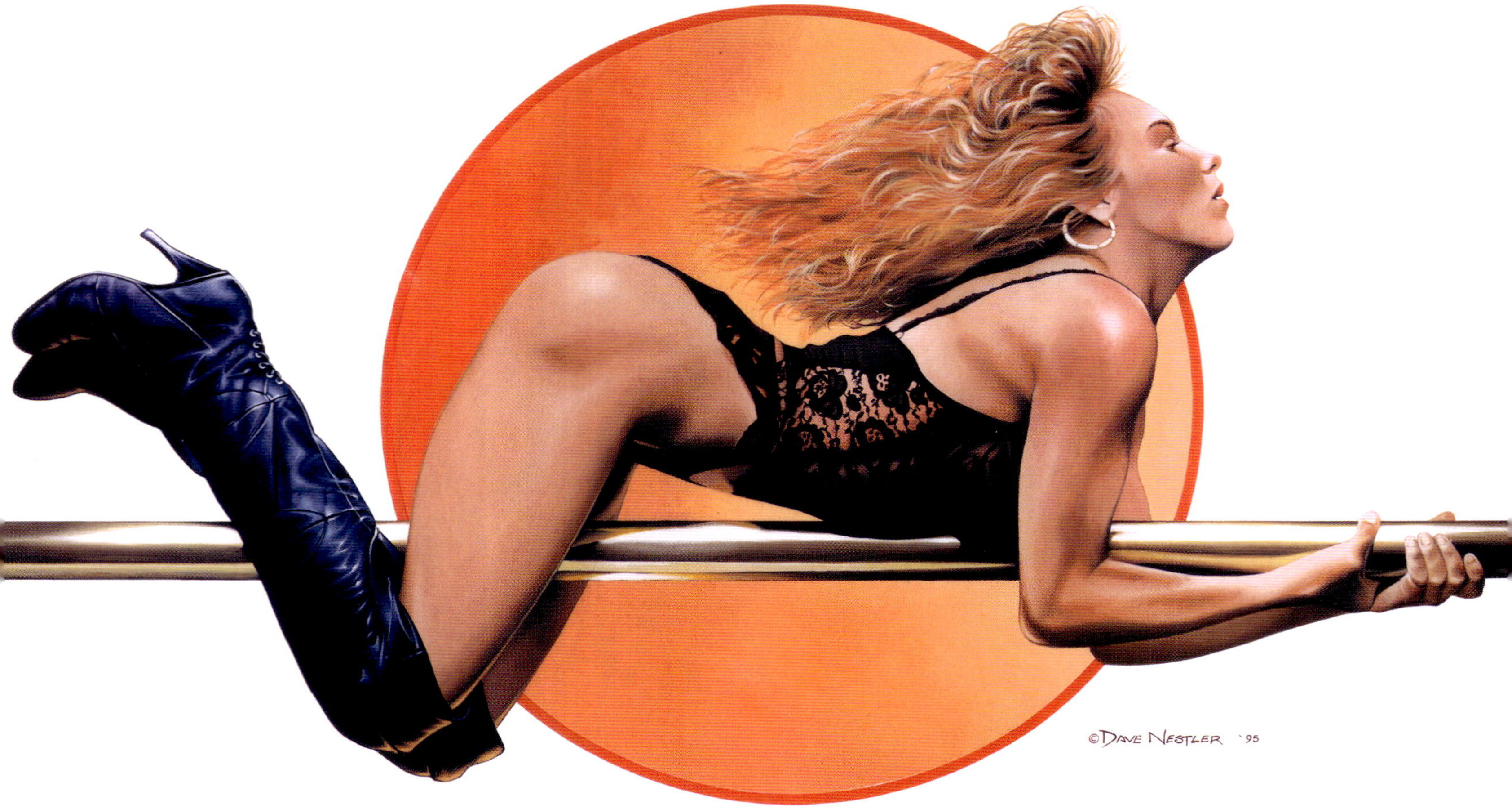

©Dave Nestler '95

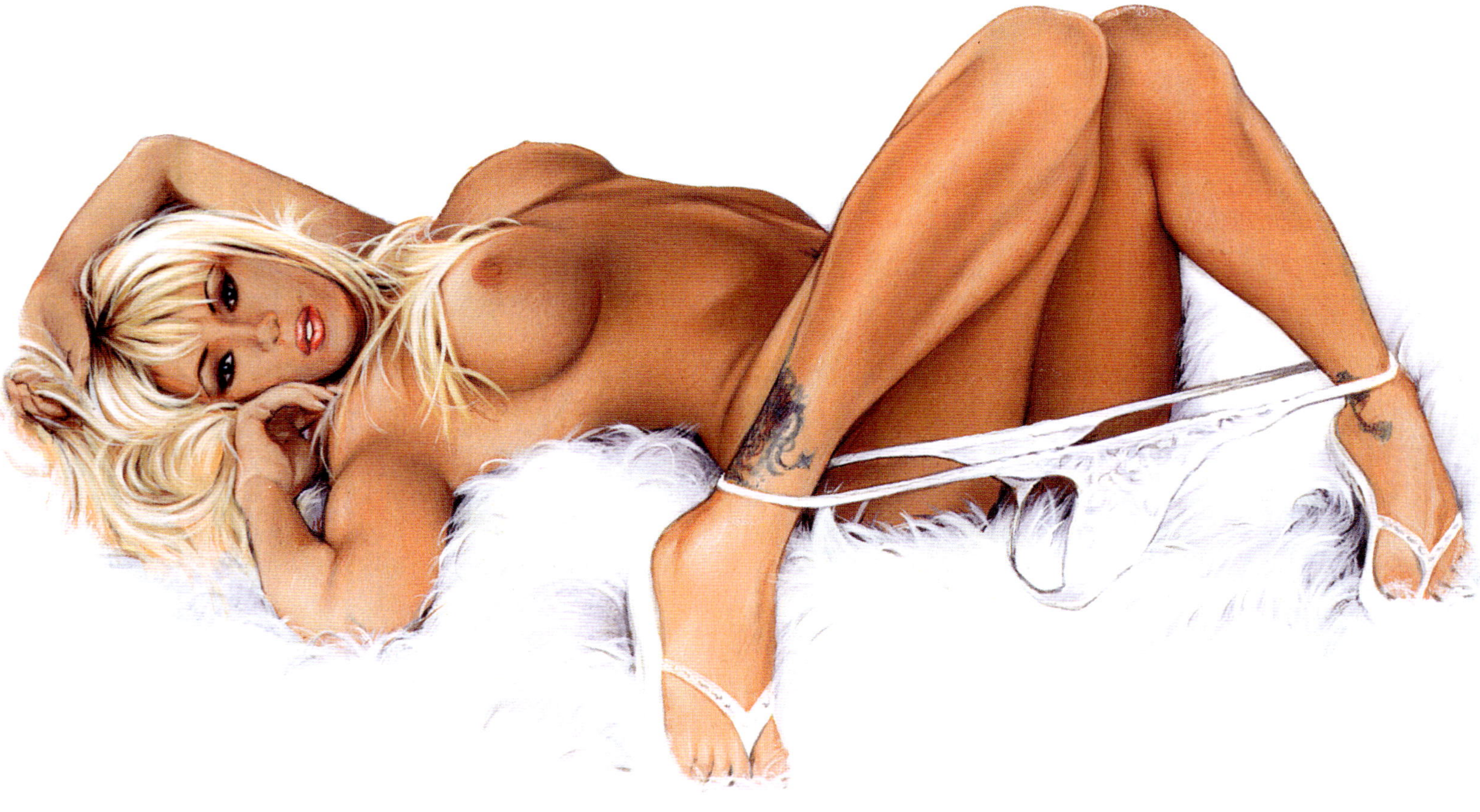

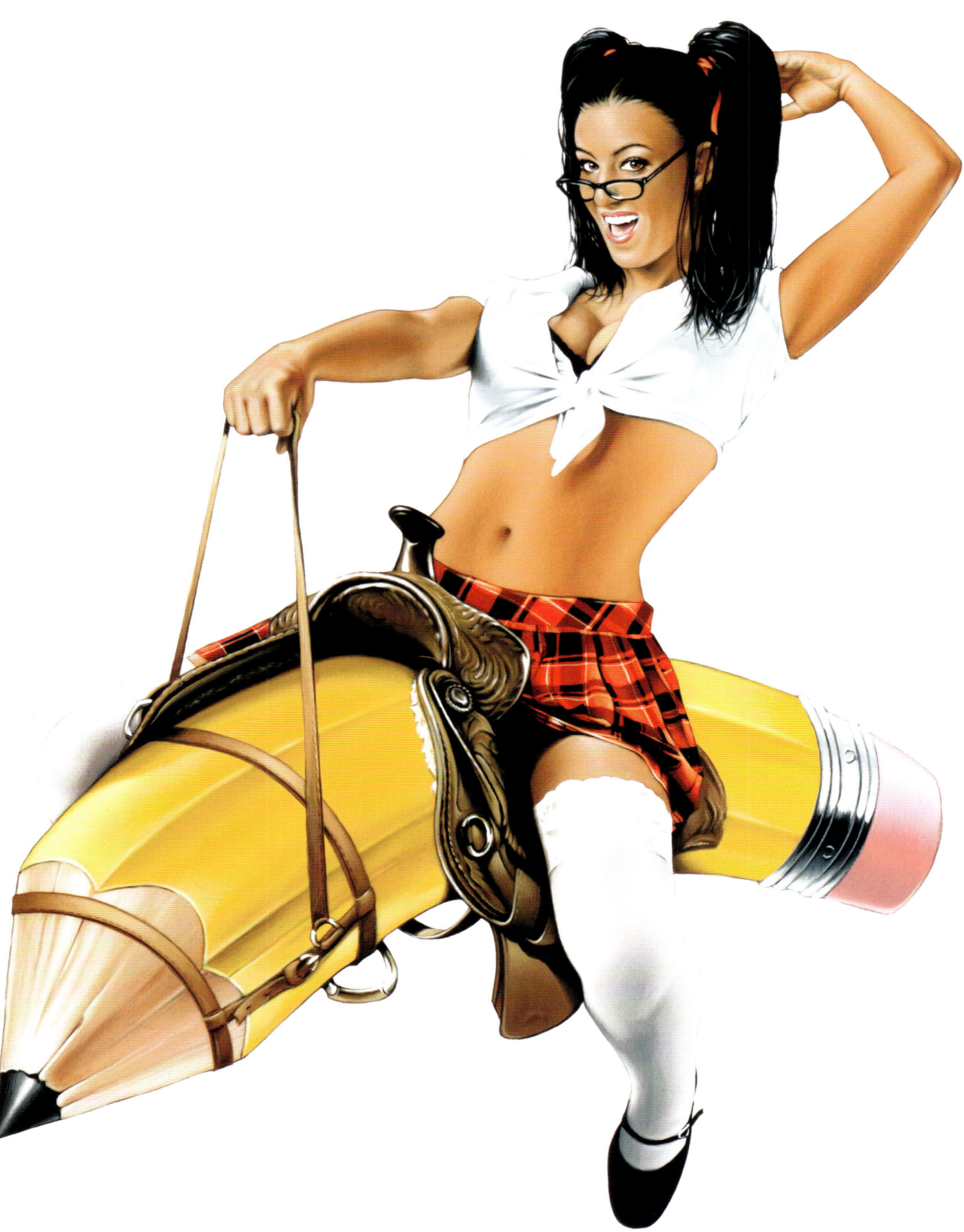

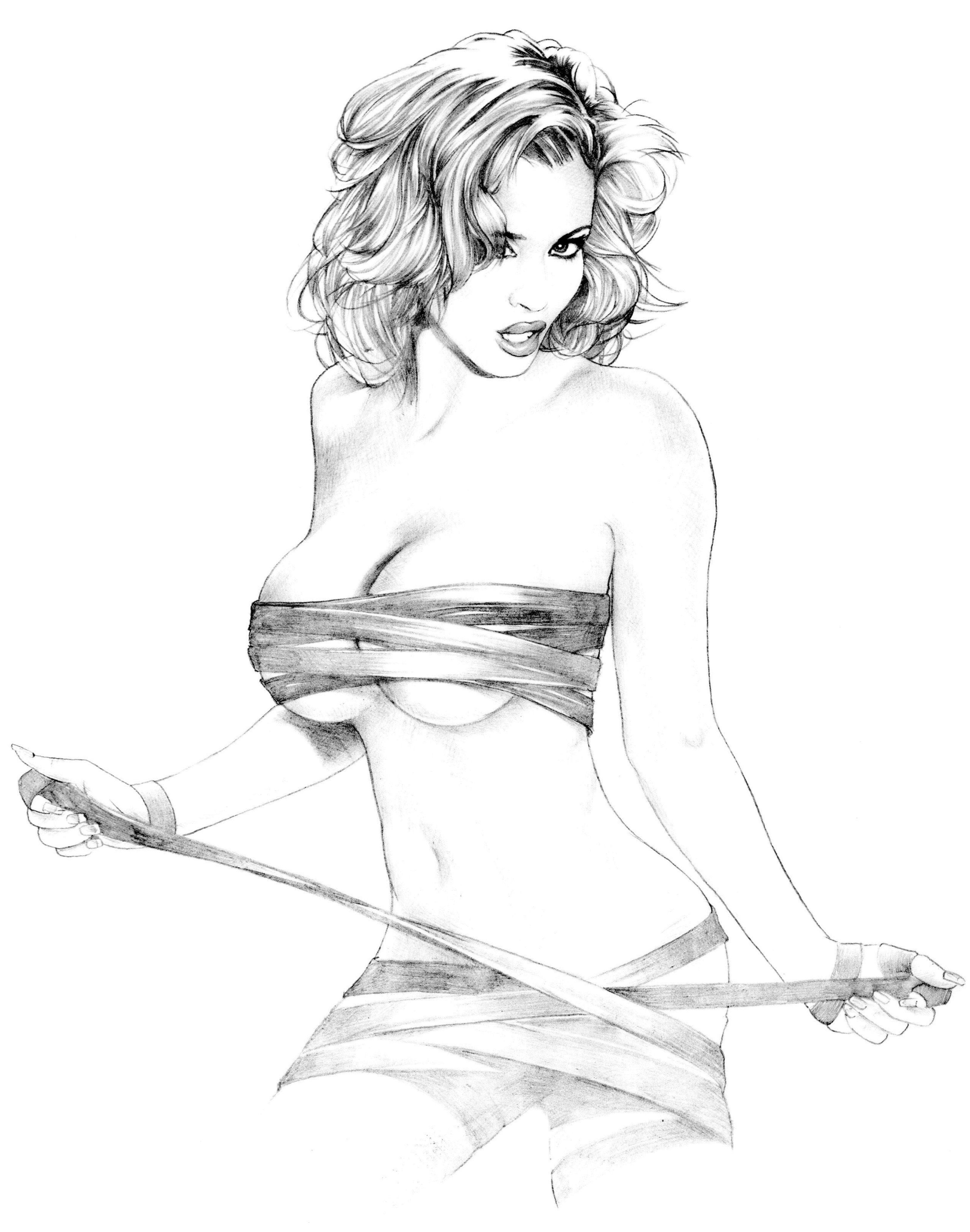

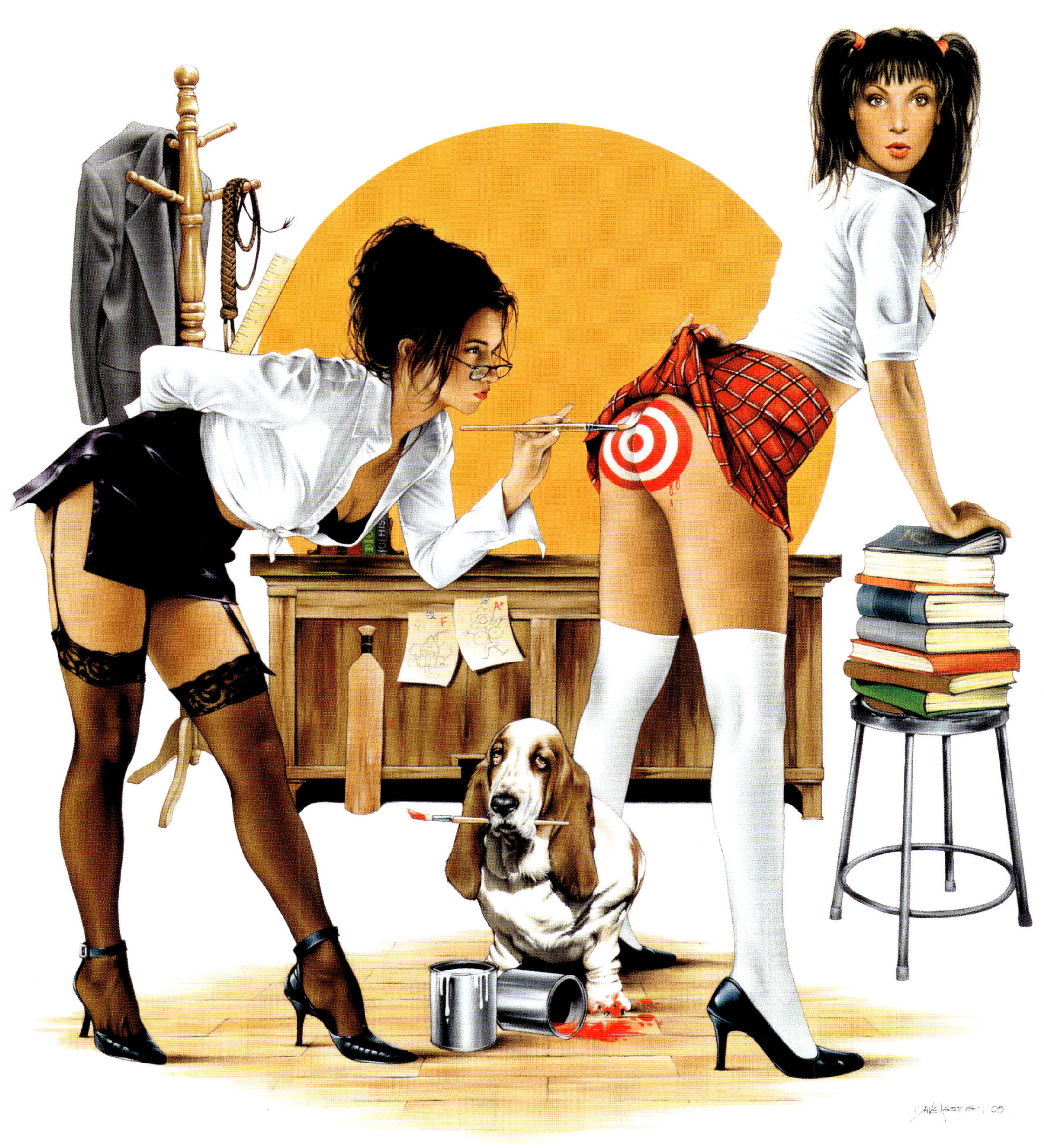

"Bored of Education"

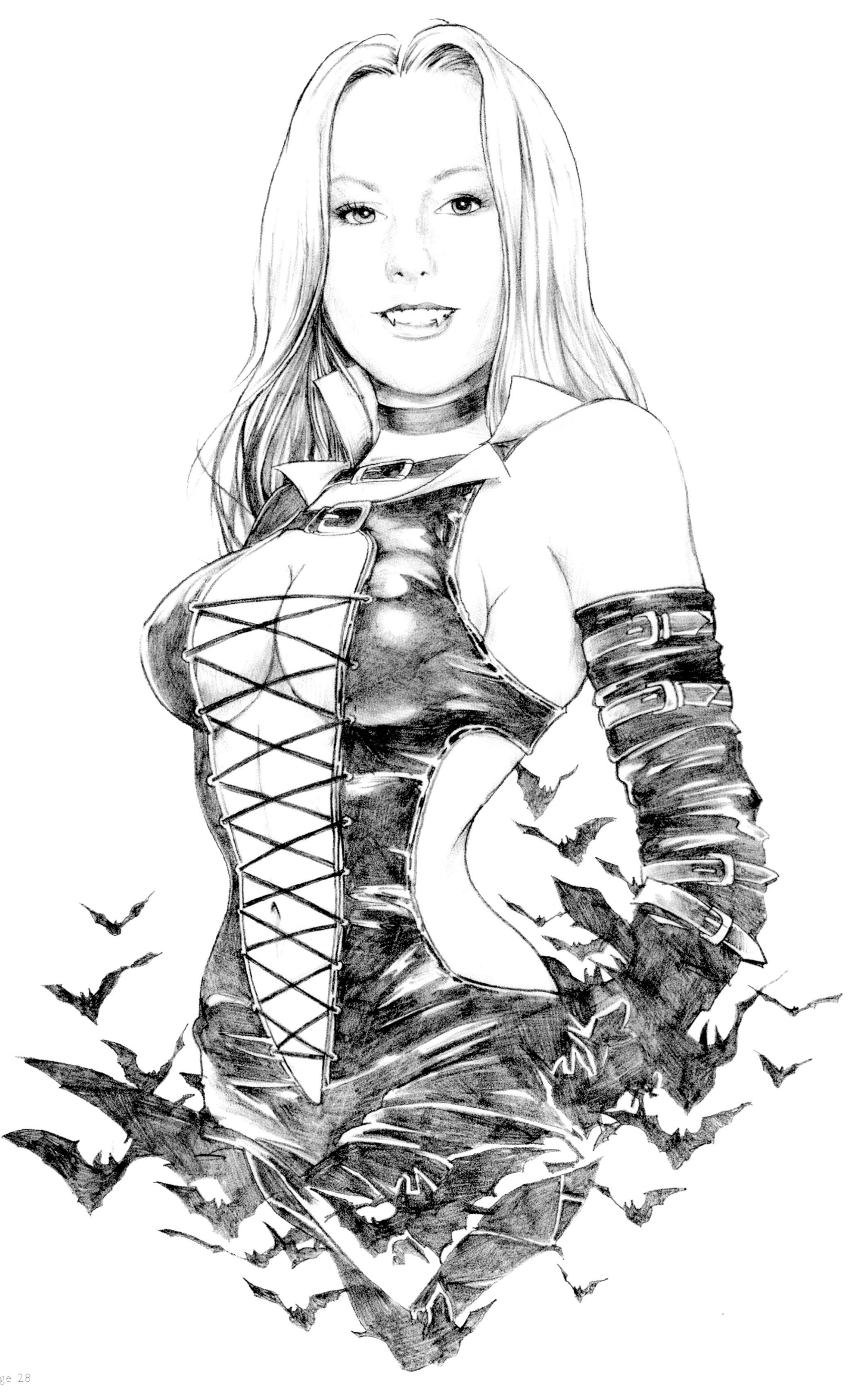

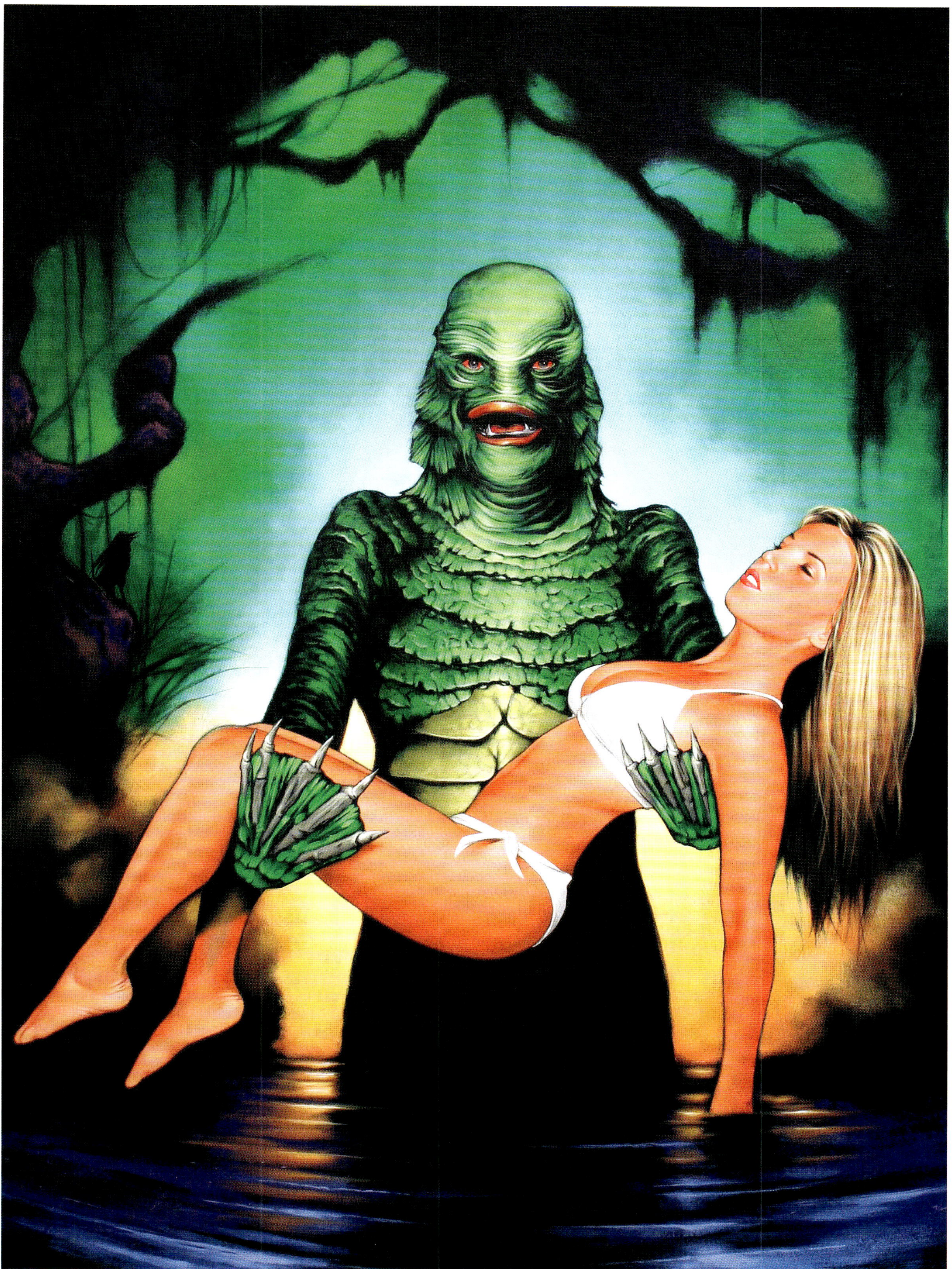

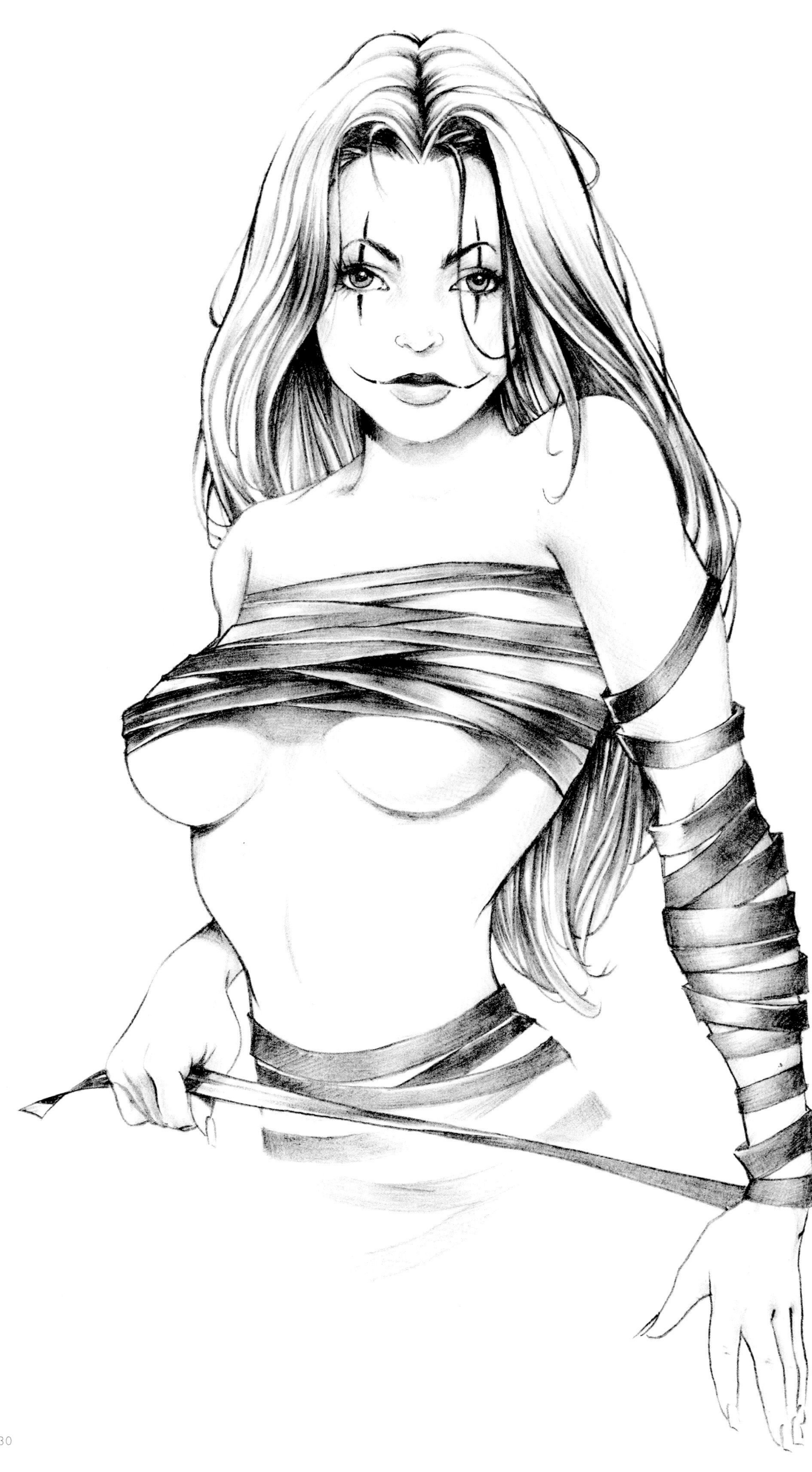

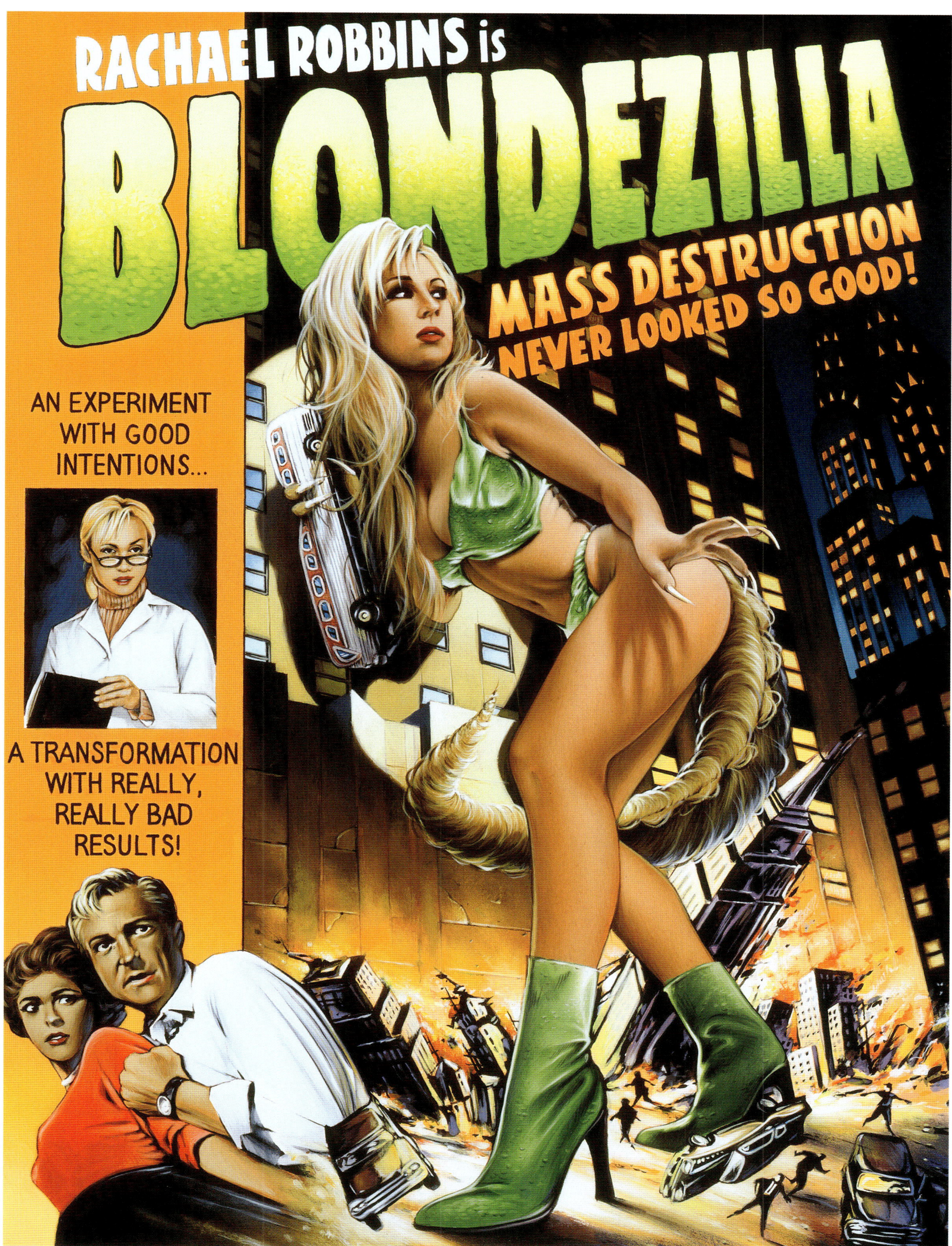
RACHAEL ROBBINS is
BLONDEZILLA
MASS DESTRUCTION
NEVER LOOKED SO GOOD!
AN EXPERIMENT
WITH GOOD
INTENTIONS...
A TRANSFORMATION
WITH REALLY,
REALLY BAD
RESULTS!

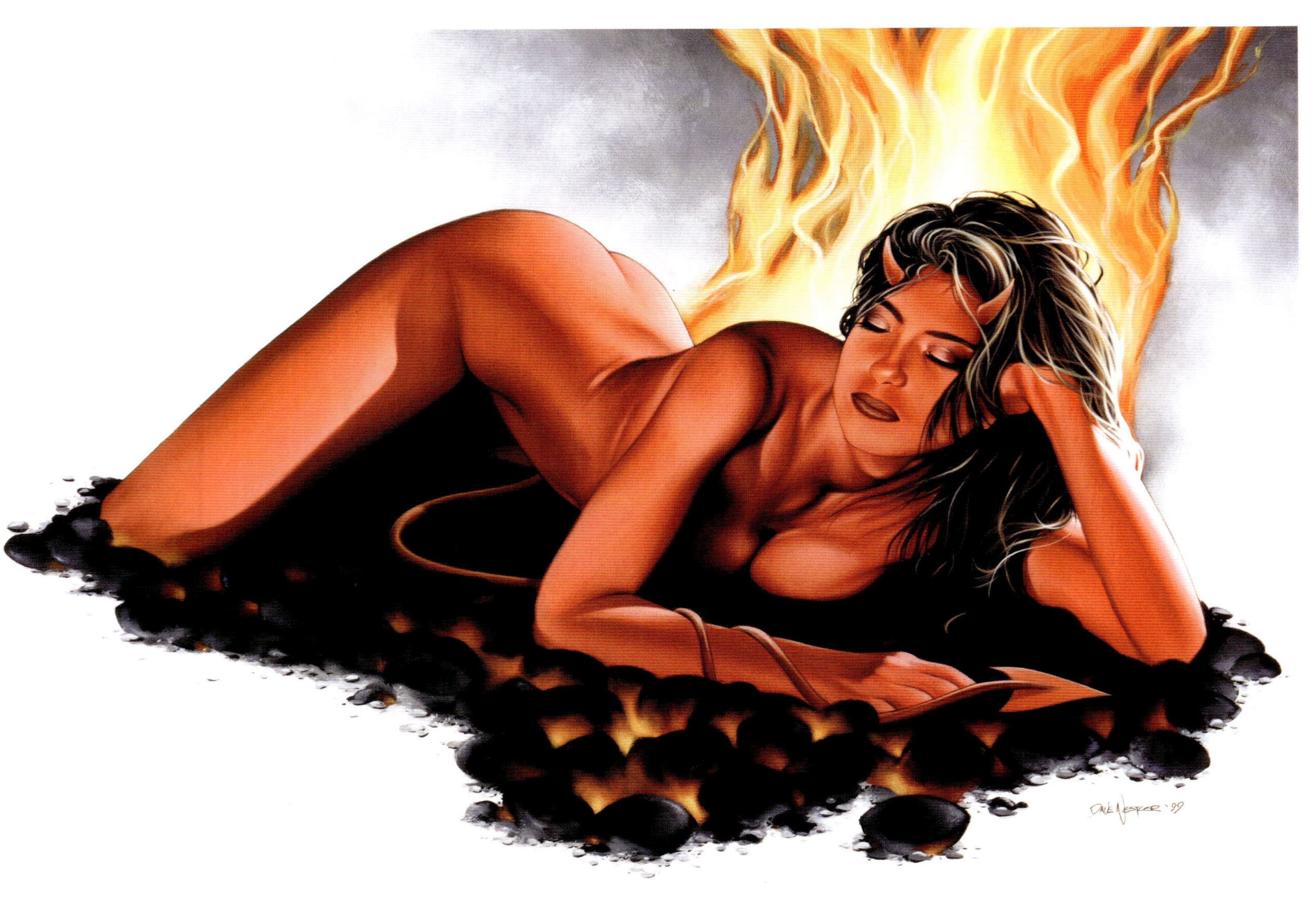

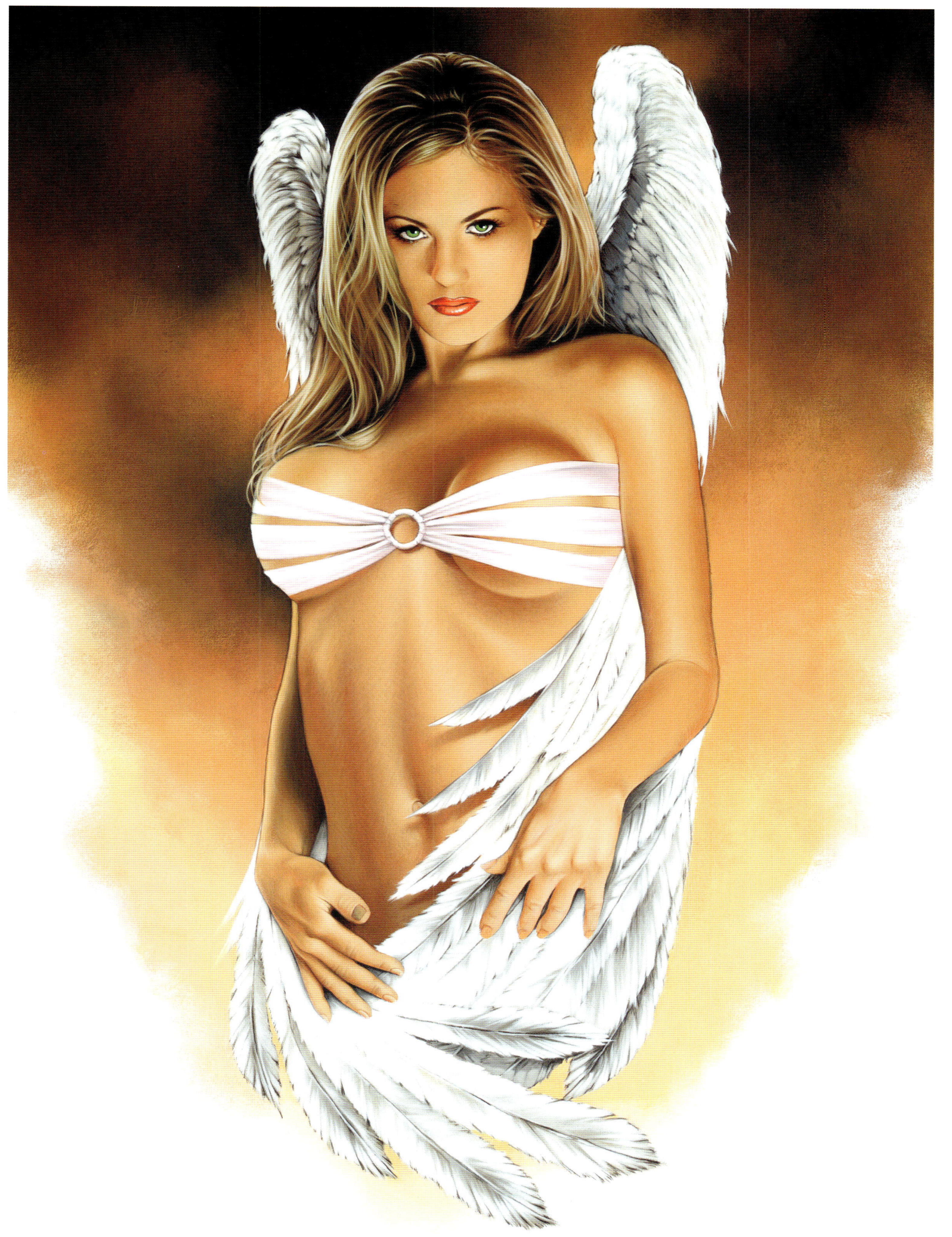

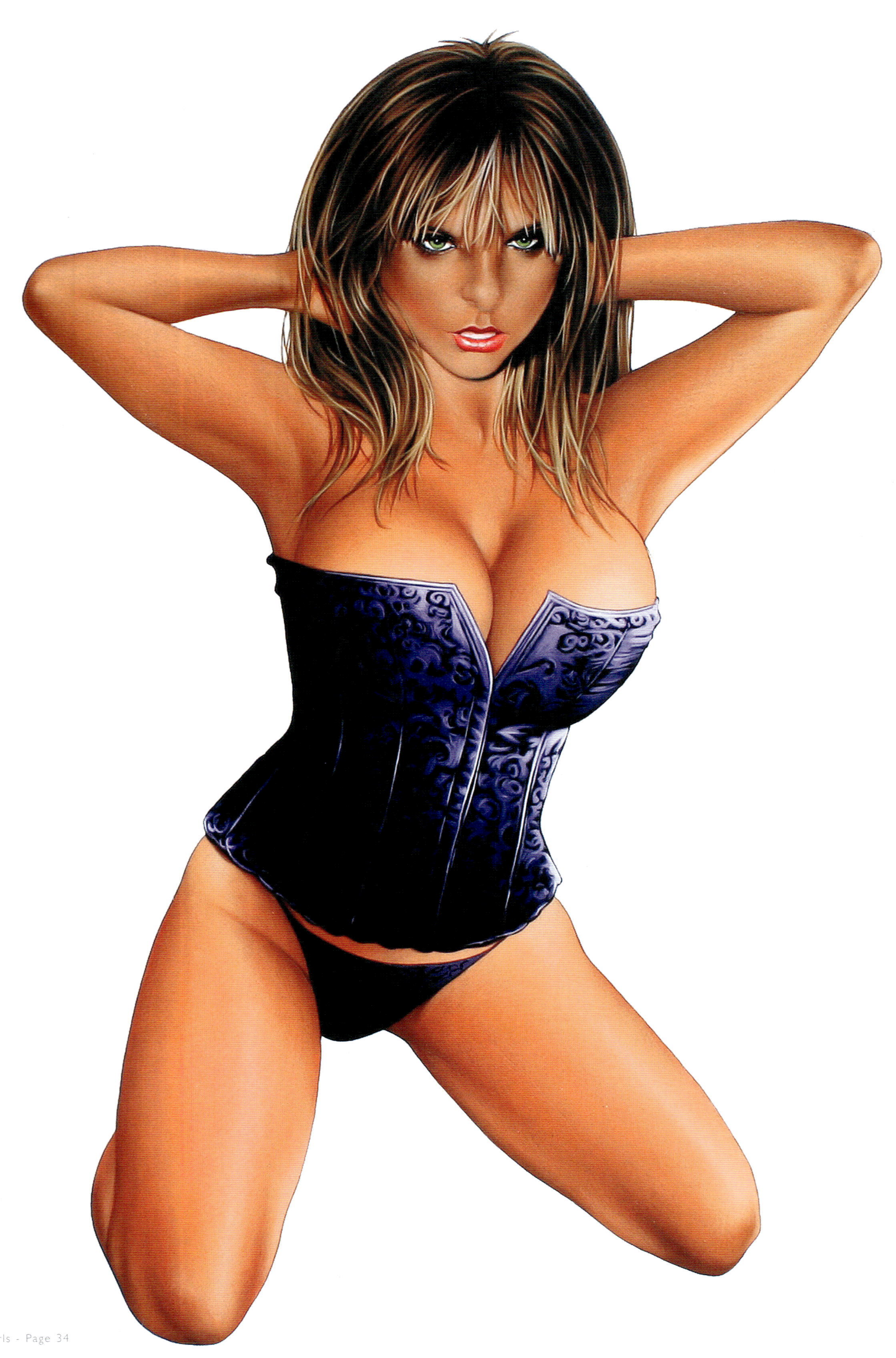

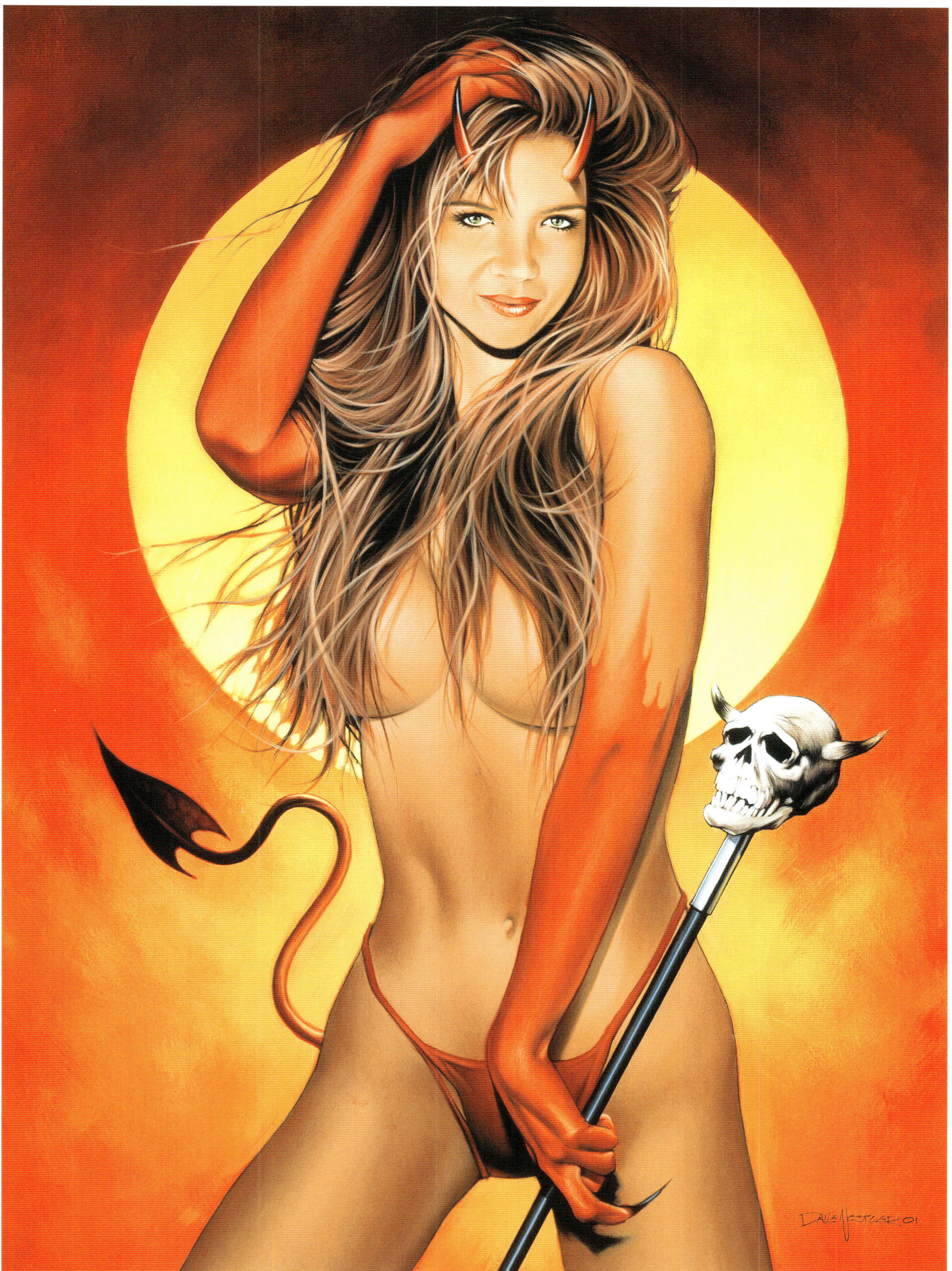

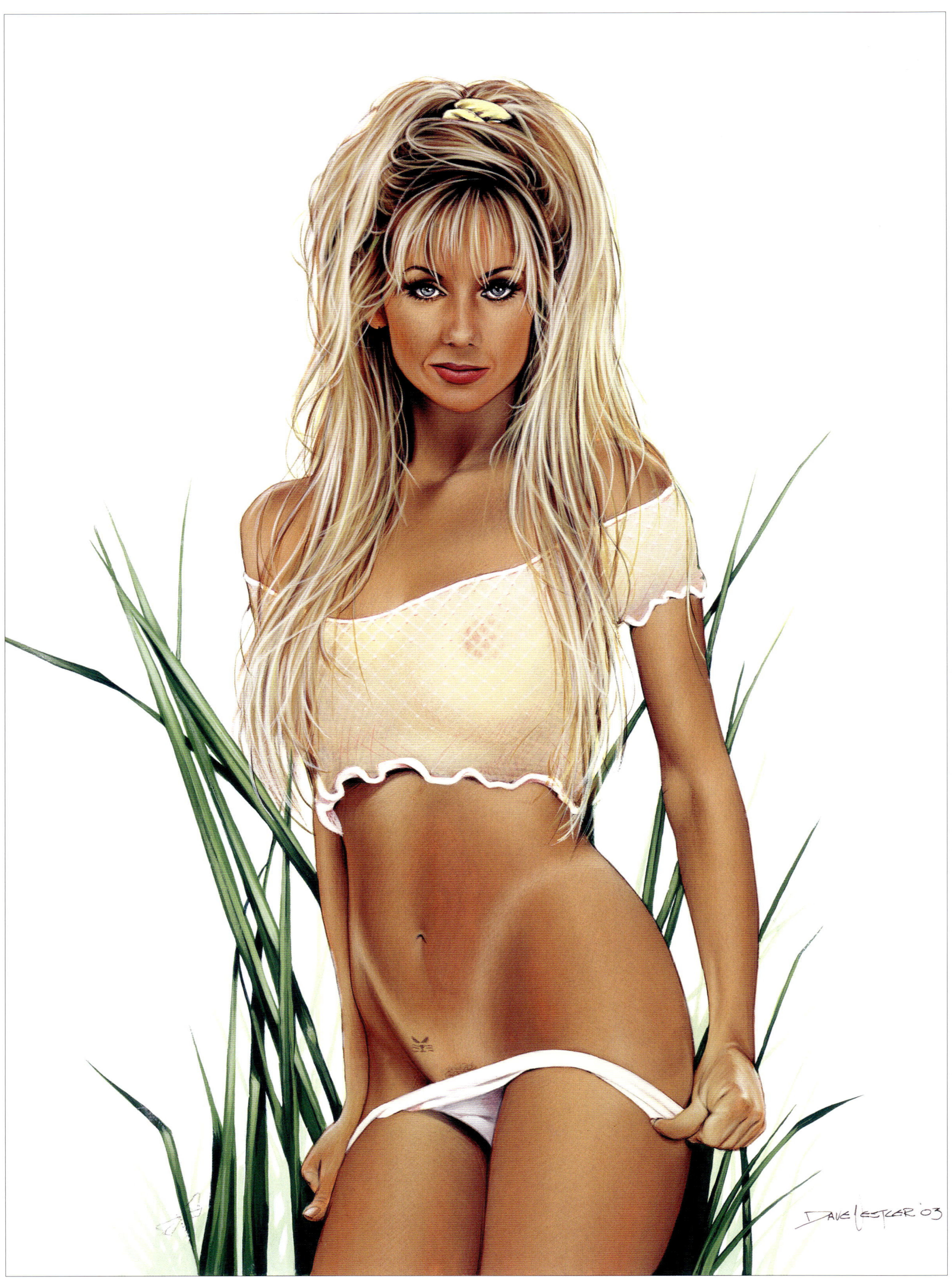
DAVE NESTLER '03

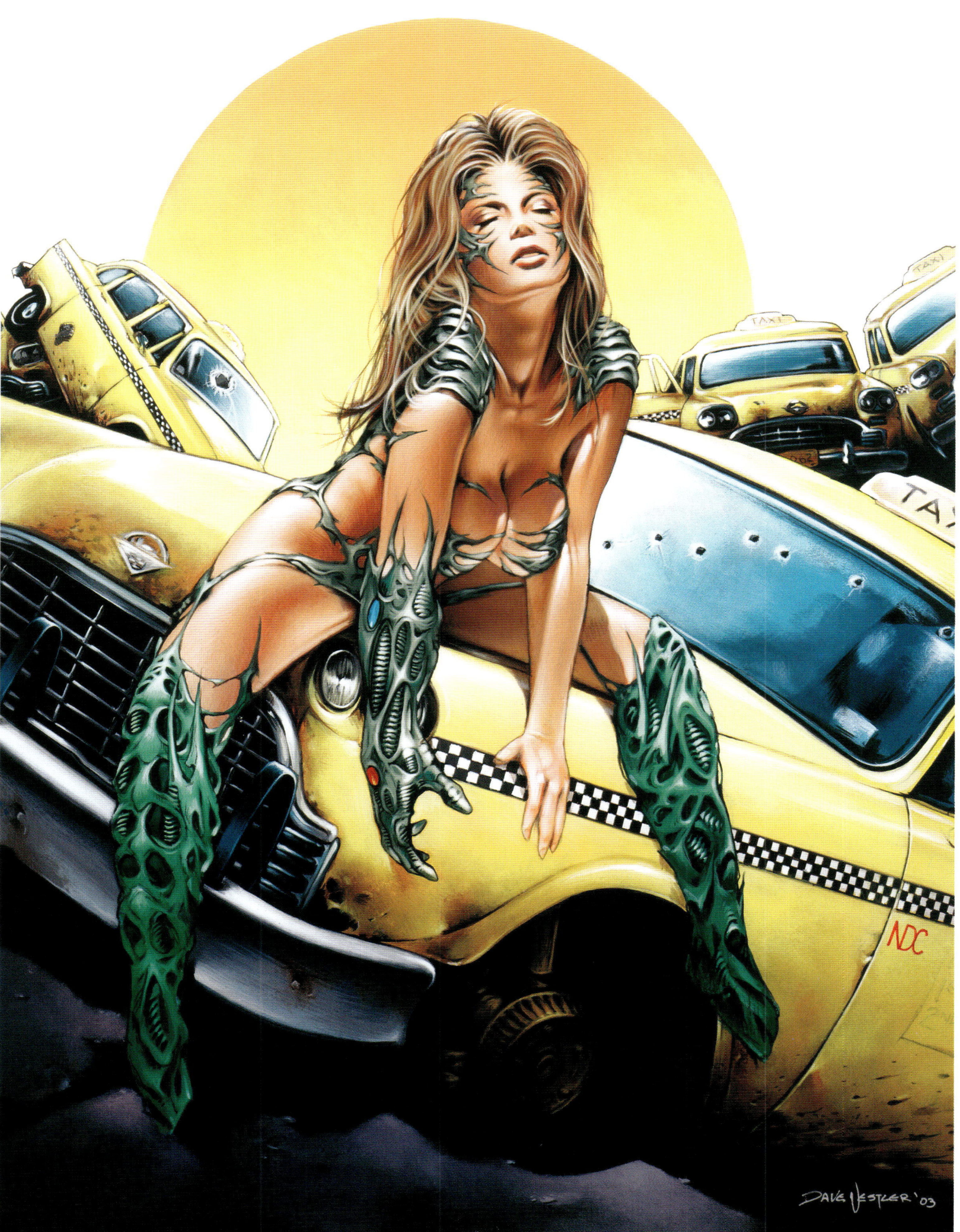
NDC
DAVE NESTLER '03

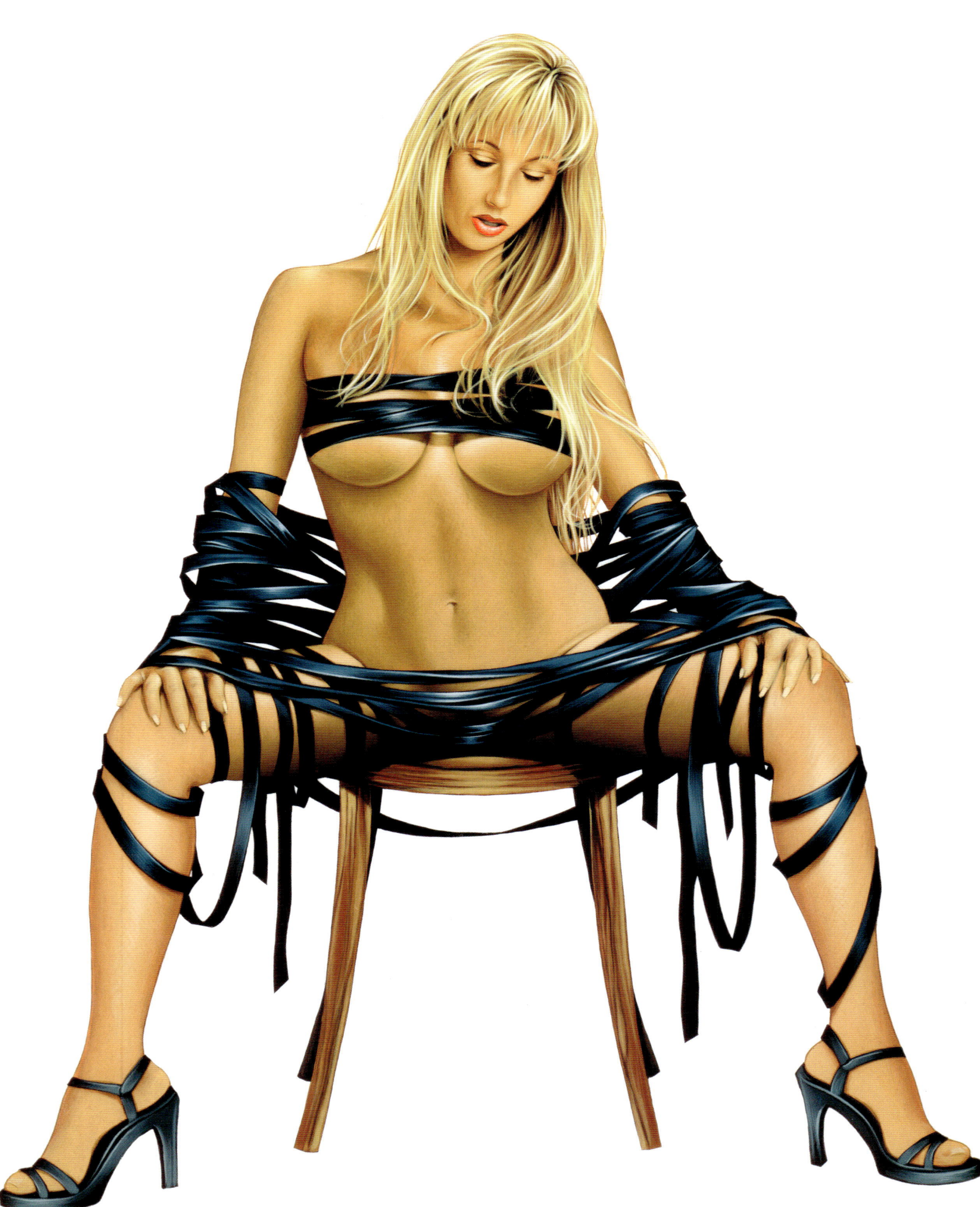

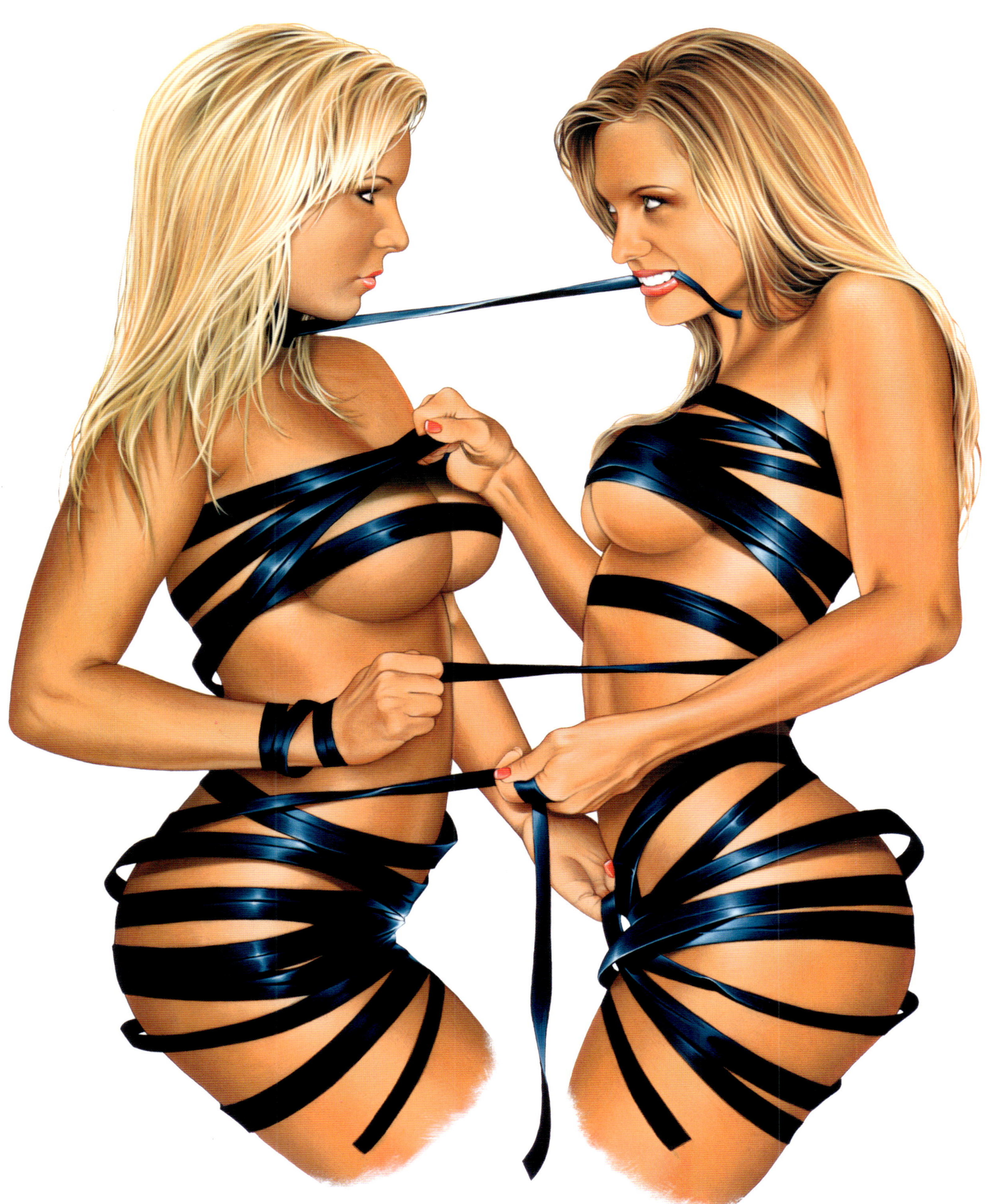

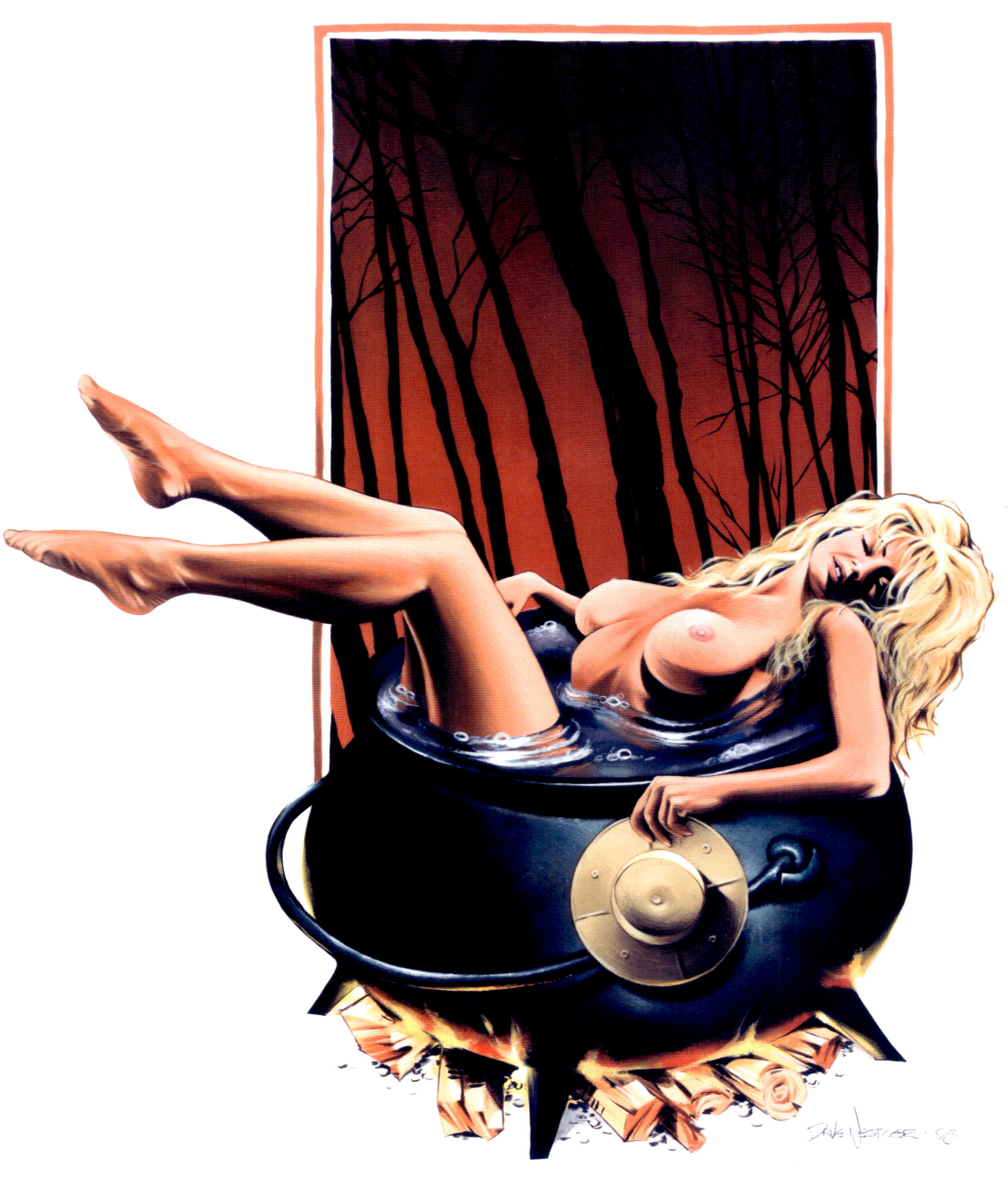

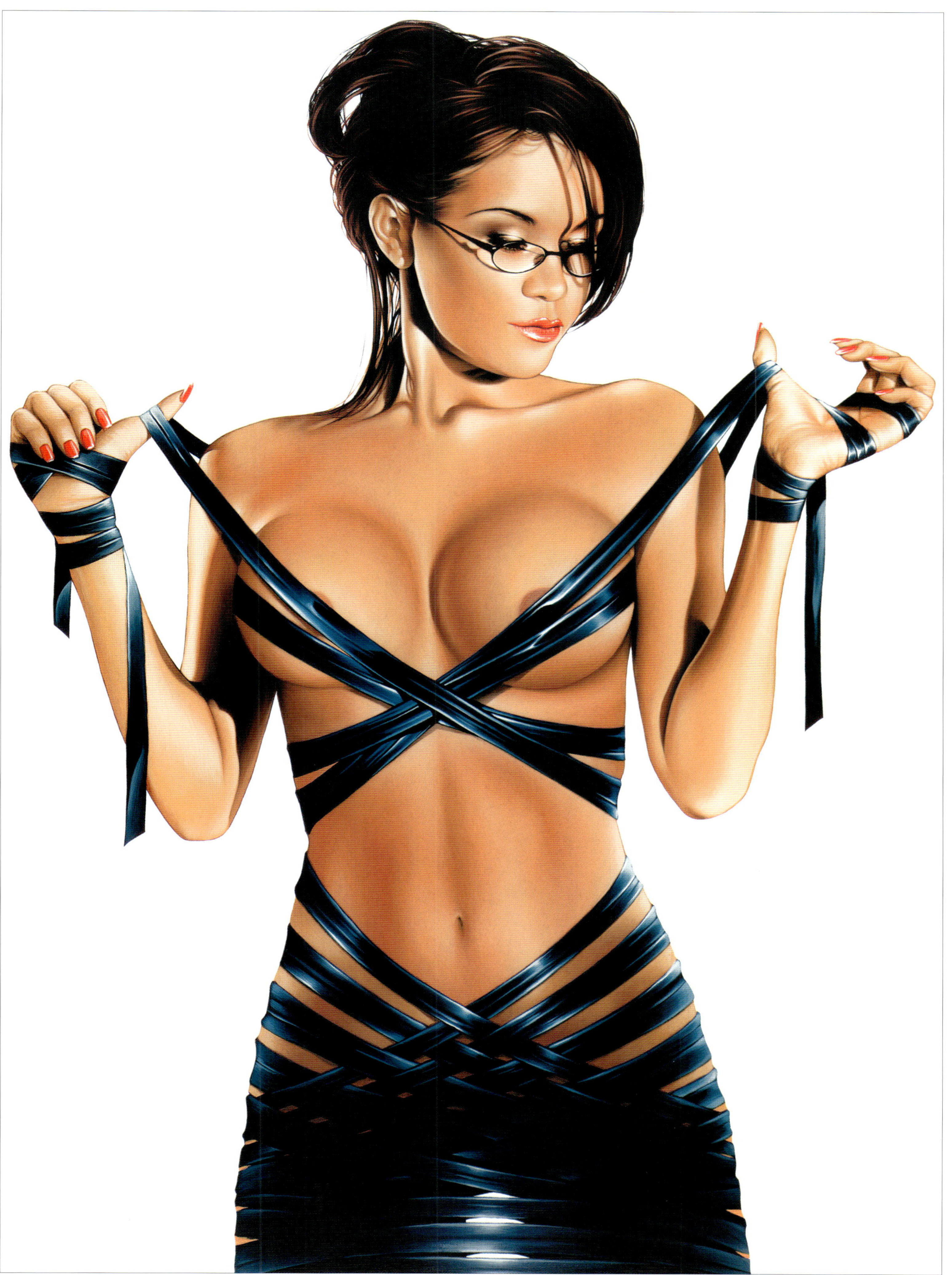

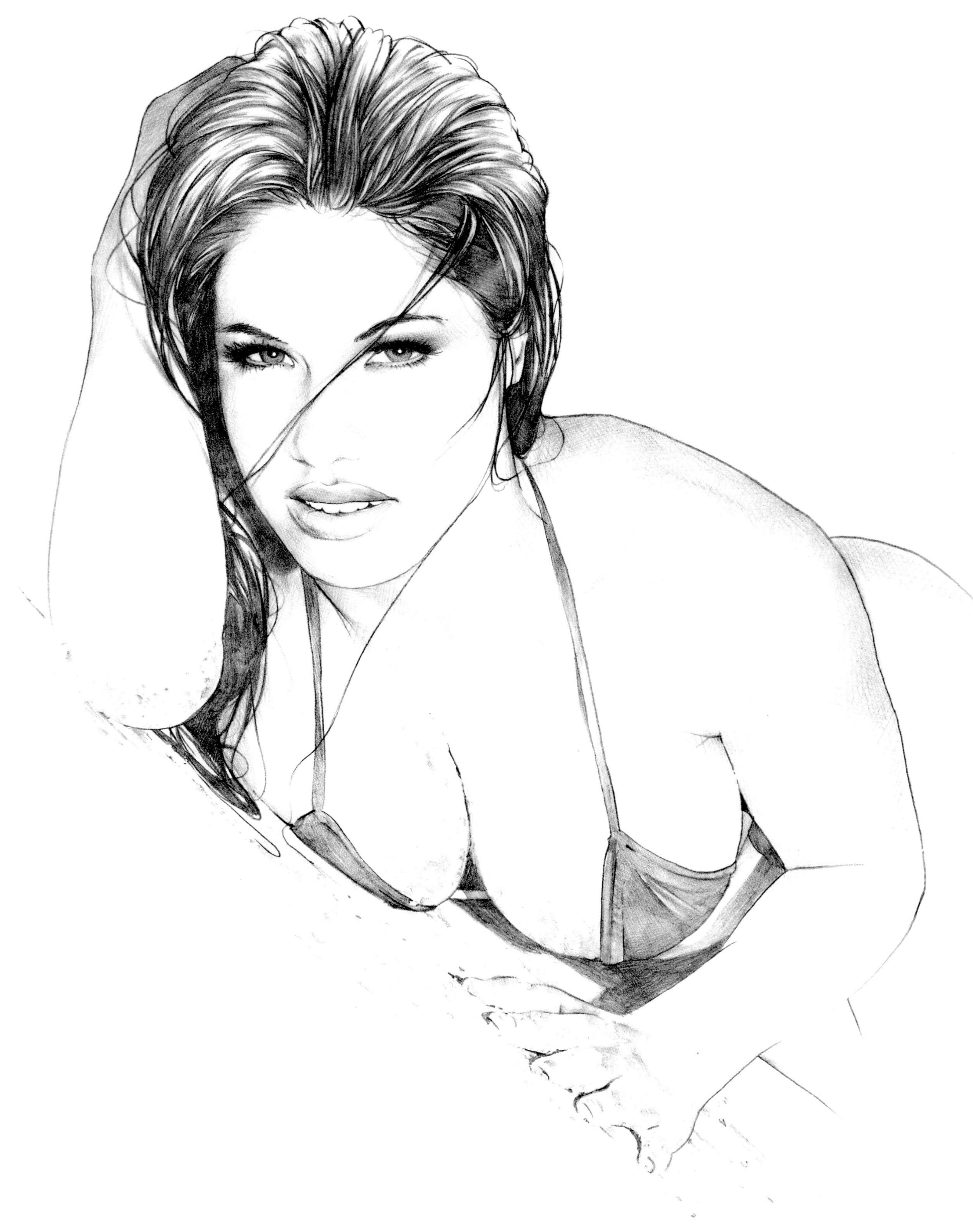

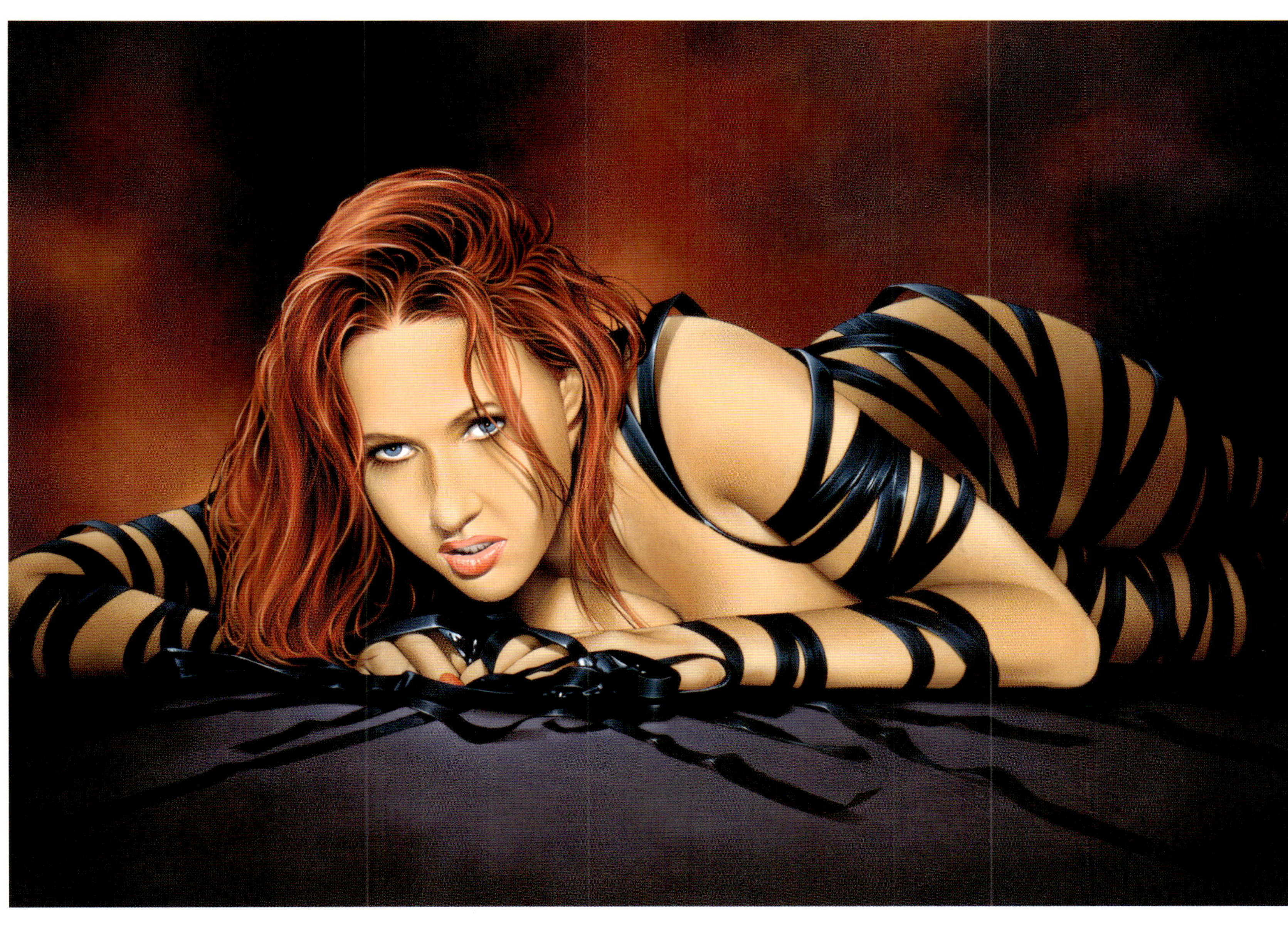

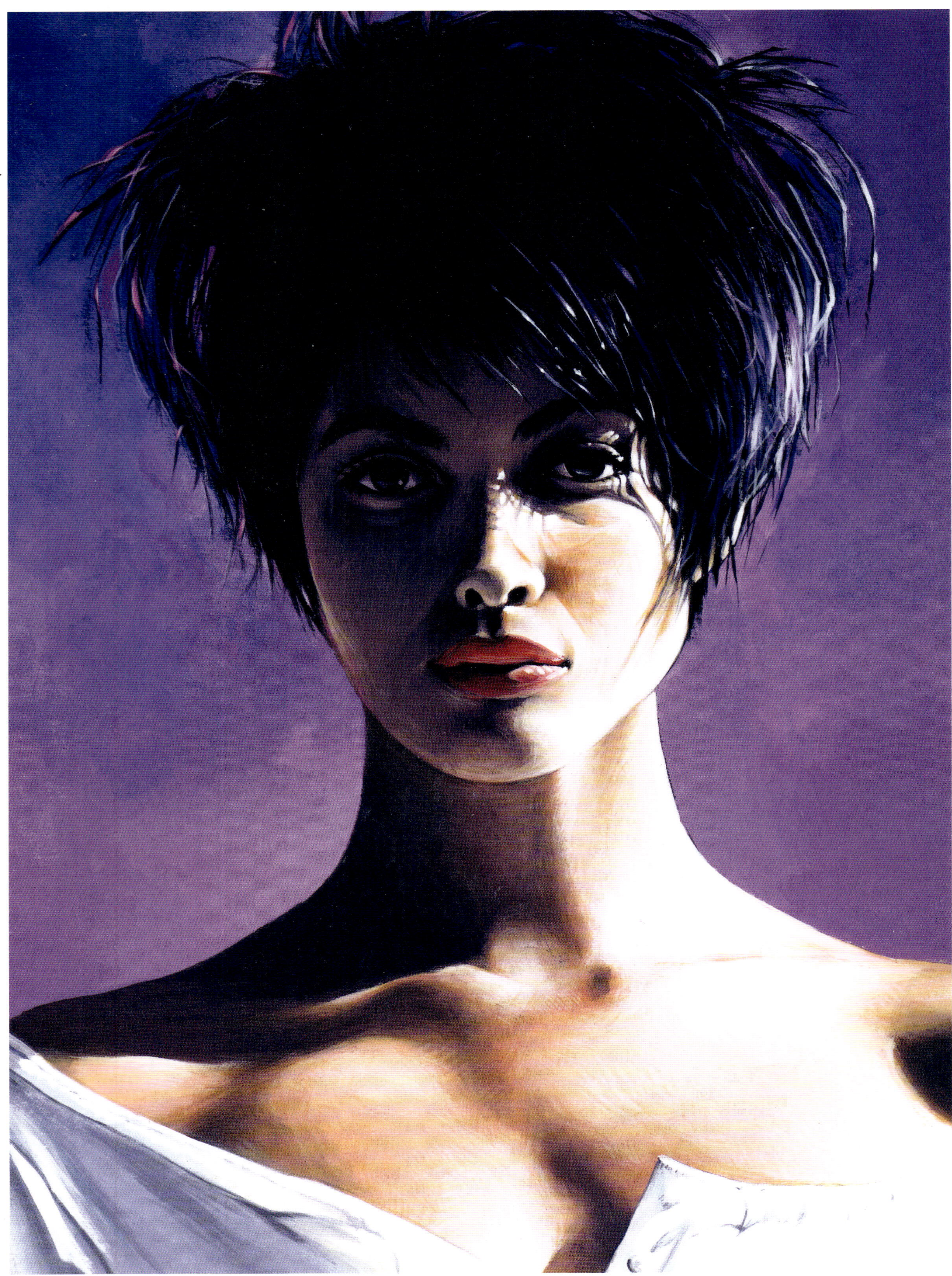

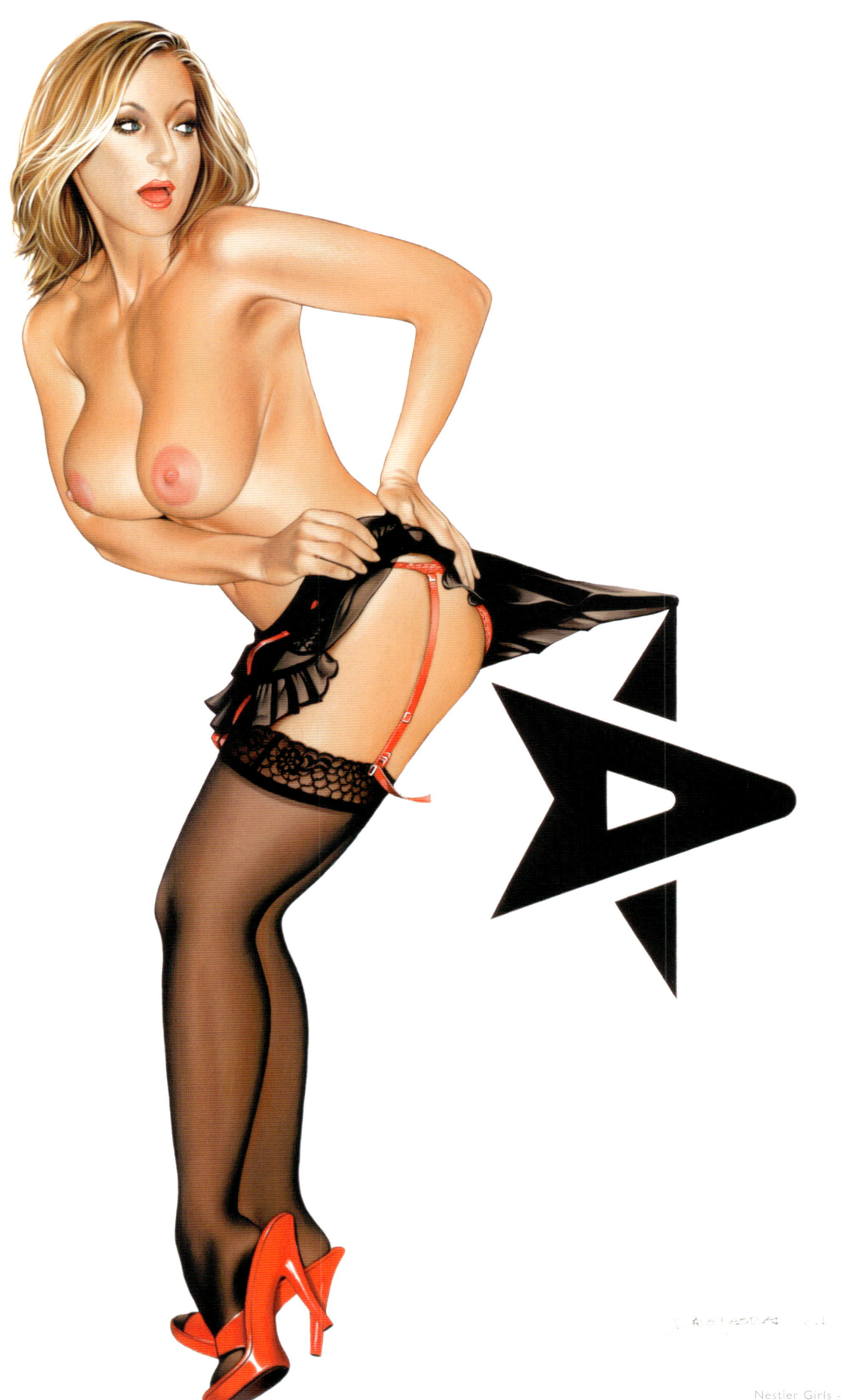

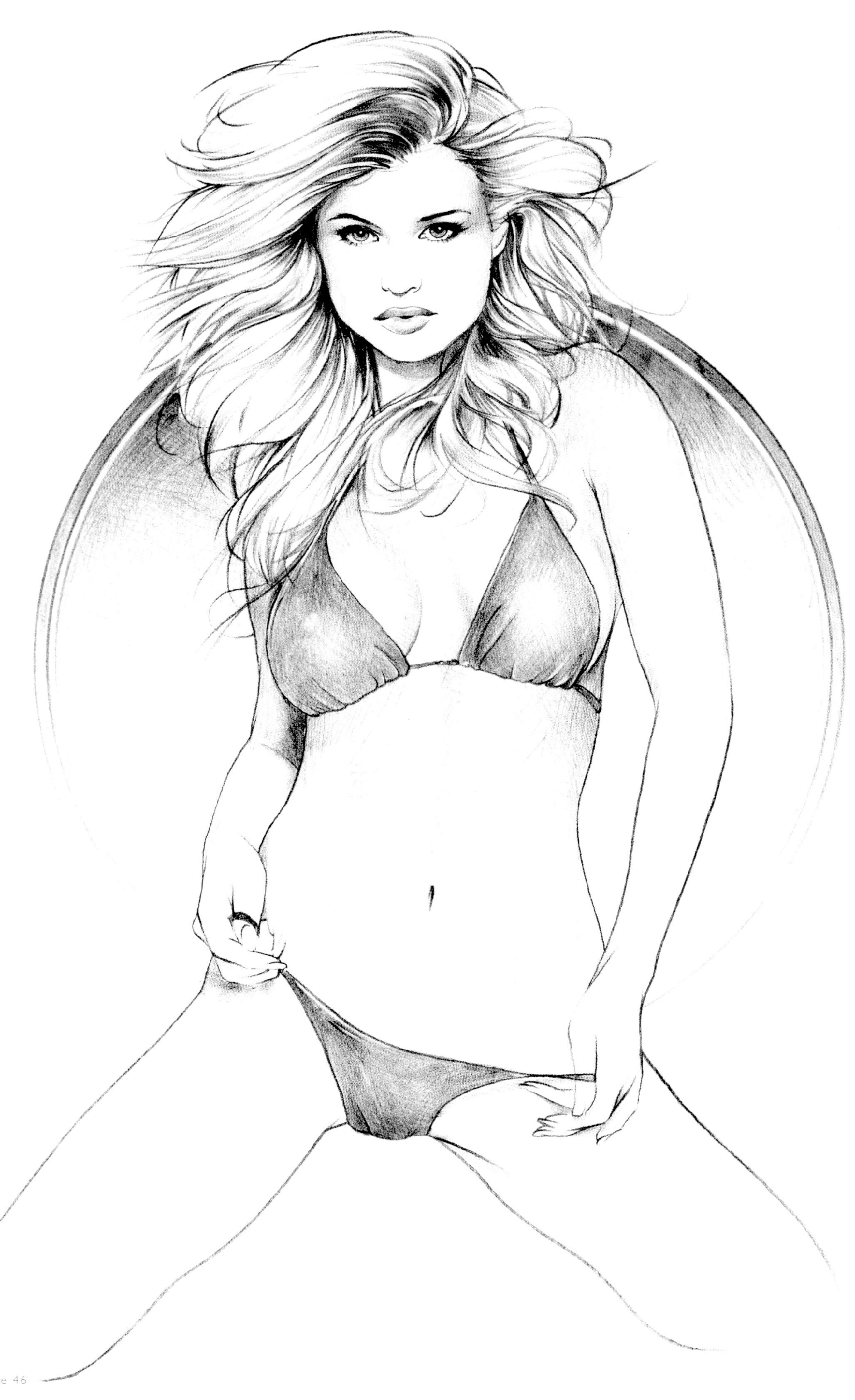

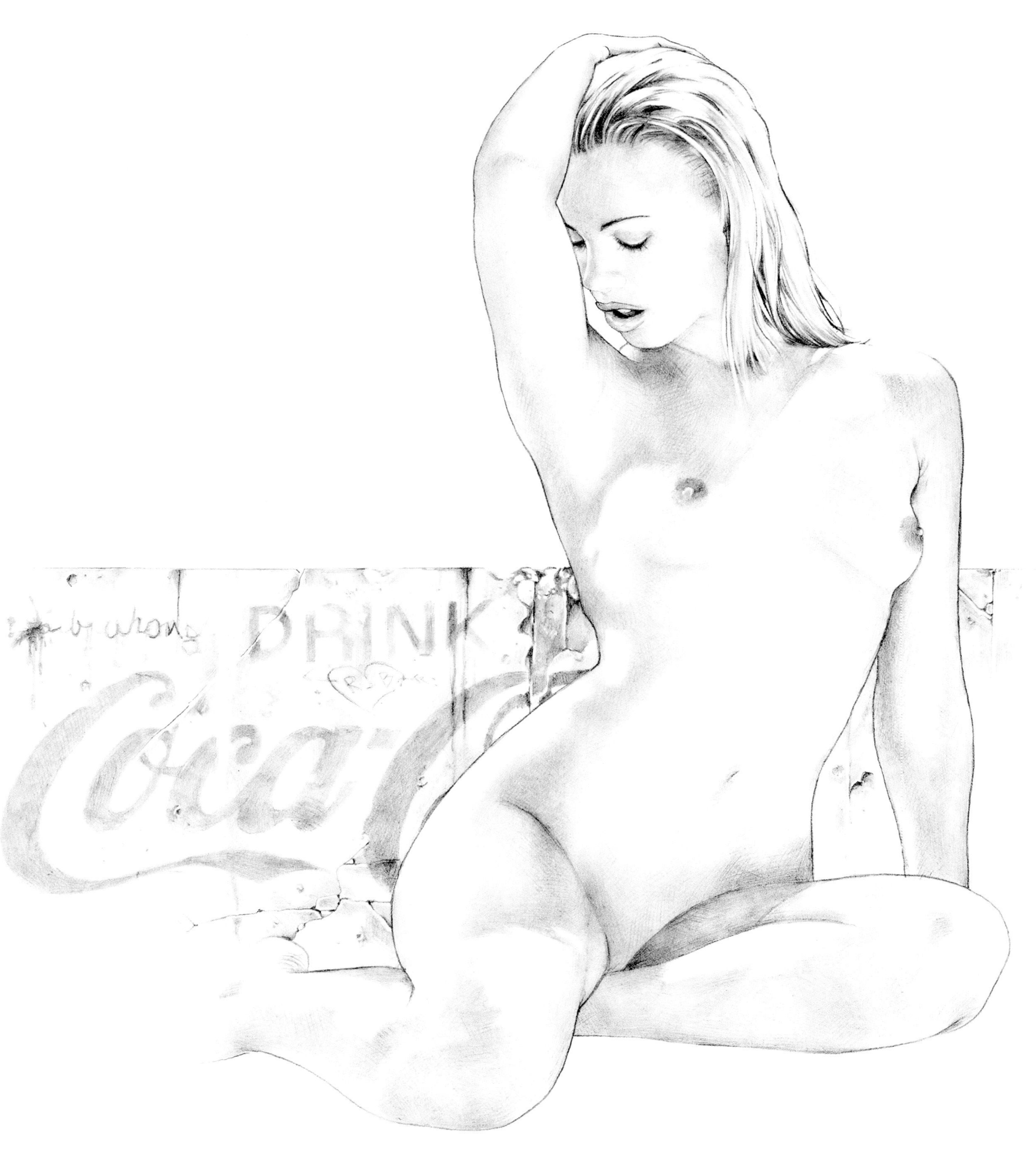
DRINK

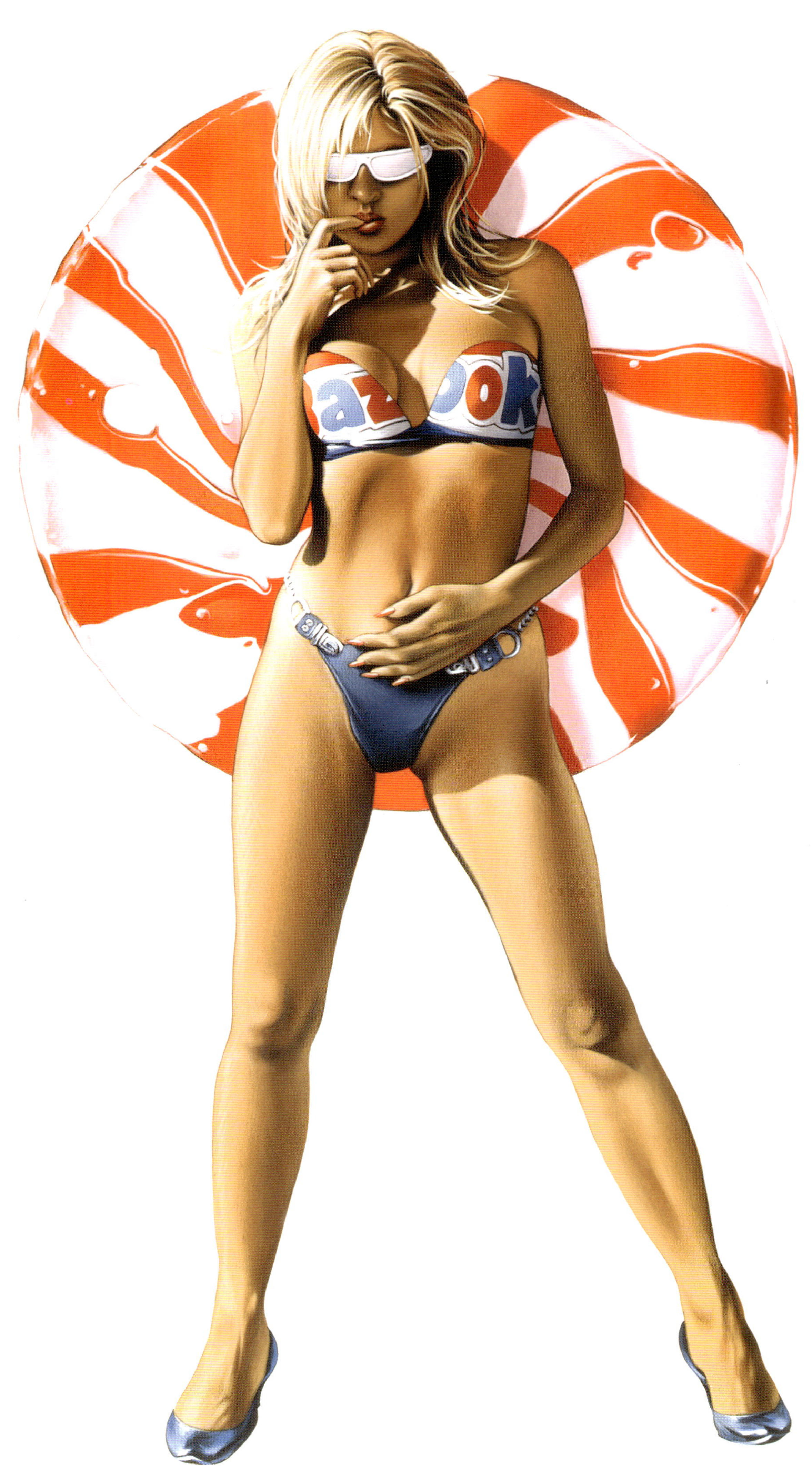